The 'Real World' Guide to Digital Filmmaking

By

Kevin B. DiBacco

Keith Publications, LLC
www.keithpublications.com
©2017

Arizona
USA

Keith Publications, LLC

Copyright© 2017 by Keith Publications, LLC
Printed in The United States of America
Contact information: keithpublications@cox.net
Visit us at: www.keithpublications.com
Gilbert AZ 85233

By Kevin B. DiBacco

Edited by Ray Dyson
www.raydyson.com

Cover art by Elisa Elaine Luevanos
www.ladymaverick81.com

Cover art Keith Publications, LLC © 2017
www.keithpublications.com

ISBN: 978-1-62882-172-7

took a few weeks. My back pain was no better; my desire to get this film done was off the charts.

This was my heavyweight championship, my one shot to get my feature film done. I knew in the back of my mind this might be the only film I would be able to direct. There were no guarantees I could even make it through a ten-day shoot on location. The crew was prepared to help me in anyway it could. We locked down our locations, set, and marked the calendar for our production date. I doubled up on my chiropractic appointments to help me get ready for this monster task.

Being on the set, the first day brought mixed emotions for me. Just a few months ago I could not get out of bed and today I was directing my first film. The power of my dream drove me to stay focused. The shoot was magical, not a fight or argument. The entire cast and crew were fully aware I was in serious pain each day. They all picked up the slack and joined my fight. They worked so hard to make this happen for me. My make-up girl Amanda would bring me ice for my back after each scene. The PAs carried around a huge recliner to place at my side. They drove this chair all over the town so I would have a comfortable place to sit. Everyone believed in me. I could not let them or myself down. Production was as hard as football camp, basic training, and the military survival school I had gone through years before. I could never describe how painful it was in words.

We finished shooting that film, *Willows Way*, and secured a distribution deal. Not only did I stay focused and battled through some very rough times, the hard work paid off. It was a hugely exciting time for me and the crew that had waited around for five years. I found myself back in the saddle, a painful saddle. It took weeks for me to recover from that shoot.

With the success of *Willows Way*, my confidence soared sky high and I decided to wait a year before I would even attempt another feature film. This time we were able to find people who would fund our film. We sold our first film, and then sold our second film, *Back to the Beyond*. Things were looking up. I had endured the largest setback in my career, or at least I thought so. I stayed committed to my art, confident I could overcome anything thrown at me.

That was until the winter of 2011. I was watching the New England Patriots in the playoffs with my family. I started felling a bit dizzy; my right eye suddenly went blurry. Was this a stroke? Did I eat too much apple pie? What just happened? I had started pre-production for my next film. I could not get sick now. The next day I went to the emergency room to find out what had happened. Some tests were run and x-rays taken. I was still on a high and in good spirits; after all, we just sold our first two feature films. The doctor come back into the room and asked me who my neurosurgeon was. I told him Dr. Florman.

He said he was calling him now. He would be right back. Moments later he walked back into the room, slid my x-ray under the light table clips and flipped the switch. He pulled out a white grease pencil and circled this big white area on the film. There was a huge mass inside my brain. Moreover, I needed to go to my neurosurgeon as soon as possible. I thought to myself: Are you serious? That was my reaction. Quickly, my high went to the lowest depths known to man. A mass in my brain? Was this life threatening? Even worse than my back? This did not only threaten my career, but was a serious medical condition. Would I be able to wiggle my way out of this one? My doctor called me later that day and made an appointment for a few days later. Rachel and I went to his office. He pulled out a massive x-ray, put it up to the light table and circled a huge mass growing from my pituitary gland.

It then occurred to me this lesson needed to be reinforced to everyone. After dinner that night, the topic of discussion was not acting, or locations or shooting the next scenes for the next day. I talked about respect. What I expected and what I will not tolerate. I made it clear that anyone acting like that again would immediately be fired, if that meant re-shooting with a different cast member I would do it. I was dead serious. From that moment on the chemistry between the cast and crew was stellar, no fights, no name calling. Everyone knew we were there for a reason, to get the film shot, and more importantly they were there to do their jobs and to do those jobs the best they can.

REJECTION AND CRITICISM

There is no way of telling our reaction to criticism and rejection until it is actually given. In my career I have always been told a project is not good enough, you can't do that, don't waste your time. Nothing feels better and motivates me more than to prove the so-called experts wrong.

I can tell you it is very hard to read reviews, especially in the low budget world. You know in your heart you could do so much better if you had more money, but you don't. Therefore, you have to make do with what you have to work with. Money is an obstacle you will always have until you have secured a huge budget to work with. You have to use rejection as a motivator. By working in this business, you invite every type of know-it-all to take a shot at you. They may criticize your work because they don't like you or your looks or that you live in a state that they don't care for. It is hard to grow a thick skin to shield yourself from people who attack your work. You have to keep critiques in perspective.

The odds are the people who are throwing you under the bus are the same people who have never attempted to make a movie or any kind of art, for that matter. If they were filmmakers they would know how hard you worked to get your film done, and criticism would be last on their mind. People like to hear themselves talk. Half the time people bash things out of ignorance, the other half of the time people just talk out of their asses. Learn to let it roll off your back. Let it make you harder and more determined.

NOTE: While writing this book, our film, *Early Grave*, was released worldwide. One of the things the writer, Mark Allen, thought would be fun was to have it reviewed by an online so called film expert. The film was out two days and the review was neutral at best. Again, by some guy who does not have a job and had never made a movie. In this case, he compares our film to *I Know What You Did Last Summer*. That film was made for seventeen million dollars. Our film, *Early Grave*, was shot and edited for less than seventy-five thousand dollars. This will happen to you all the time. How can they compare a movie that cost two hundred times more to make? The good news I can take from this review is that he did like our film better.

TRUE STORY:

Imagine you make your very first feature film. Use all the funds you have available, get it made, the film is picked up by a distributor, and sold around the world. You even get the film picked up by Netflix, the ultimate indie filmmakers' goal. What could be better, right? You are riding high. Three months later, you begin to read the reviews. People are comparing your film to *Star Trek* or *I am Legend* or *Transformers* even. They are comparing your small movie to these one-hundred-million-dollar behemoths and bashing everything about your film from acting to special effects. All the while, you know your film was produced for less than what Hollywood spends on bottled water for the cast and crew. That is exactly what happened to me once *Willows Way* was in distribution. This labor of love was torn apart by people comparing our film to these mega budget Hollywood films. Honestly, I was not prepared for that. I was sure viewers knew the difference between low budget indie films and the big budget Hollywood films.

No they don't.

The average viewer has no clue if your film was shot in video or film. Viewers go by who is in the film. Like the average TV viewer, you are dealing with people who are numb.

The budget didn't matter. They rented our film and it did not have digital effects like *Transformers* or *Resident Evil*. I was crushed, I was angry; I had all kinds of different emotions. Eventually Rachel convinced me I did the best with what I had.

Having your film bashed will hurt. Having your film bashed by people who don't even know how to make a film will piss you off. You will find everybody is an expert.

You have to learn to have a short memory. Yes, a short memory like an NFL quarterback. The old saying is that when a quarterback throws an interception he has to have a short memory. Meaning he has to forget about it quickly and move on.

Remember that rejection and criticism are an everyday occurrence, in everyday life. Colonel Sanders was rejected one-thousand-and-nine times when peddling his now famous chicken recipe. Twelve publishing houses ejected J.K. Rowling and Walt Disney was turned down three-hundred-and-two times for the financing of Disney World. Rejection happens to everyone so don't quit learning how to accept and build character from it.

YOUR SUPPORT NETWORK

Even before you think about working in this business or taking on a project like making a movie, ask yourself what is my support network? My wife? Girlfriend? Boyfriend? Father? Mother? Will they support my dream? Do they understand what it means to fully commit to an art project that has no guarantee of making money?

Despite what others may think, you cannot make a movie on your own. It is a team game. Even with your team behind you, you are going to need the support of your family and friends. Without a good support system backing you, making a feature film is impossible.

TRUE STORY:

Early in my career when I started working in this business, I never stopped to ask myself this very question. Not being married, and living the single life it never occurred to me that you need help to achieve any type of goal. You are only as good as your supporting cast. That means you need help. So when I met a nurse who made a great salary I instantly thought this was perfect for me. She had a nice house, and was a nursing supervisor in one of Connecticut's nicest hospitals. I would be able to keep shooting my late-night music videos with local bands. Make some money with my art and making my way as a director. I could not have been more wrong. It started out great. It wasn't long before I was getting flack for coming home late from my cable-TV production job, then going out to shoot music videos. It became an issue. I didn't understand. This was really what I wanted to do. I love to shoot and edit. Why can't we get together once or twice a week? What I didn't realize is that I had no support from the very person I thought would let me do my thing. Dinner at six, weekends spent at flea markets, getaways to Vermont. Maybe I was just with the wrong girl. Surely, they can't all demand that much time when I am trying to build my career. That relationship burnt out, then another, then another, then another.

Was it me? How can I accomplish my goals and be asked to commit so much time to a relationship? It took some time for me to understand it was one or the other. I didn't need support from a girlfriend, I had to motivate from within, follow my heart. Here I am a twenty-something shooter and editor, had my first music video on MTV and no support whatsoever from the woman in my life. I soon realized the women I met, while intelligent and established, did not understand the life of the indie filmmaker. Being in a bar and shooting a music video with a bunch of painted up, drunk guys and girls just kept their minds racing. They did not understand it was part of what I do.

You need to understand a support system is key when you are trying to create art, film or video. Once I got to my thirties I began to date women who were more into the arts themselves. I began to find an entirely different feel for what I did. There was less pressure to conform to the 9 to 5 lifestyle. However, it was a rough go. I was called everything from a dreamer to a bum with no real future. Many of my girlfriends and their parents just did not get it. The moral of this story is before you begin this business take your boyfriend, girlfriend, wife or husband aside and tell them your goals; make sure they support you 100 percent. If not you will have to deal with the battle at home as well as all the other problems you have to deal with in life. Your significant other needs to be on board with you. Odds of success are very slim if you do not have that support system in place.

CHAPTER 2

FUNDING

Making movies is not for the poor; don't fool yourself before you even start. It costs money to make a movie and it costs money to sell a movie. That being said, the entire reason for writing this book is to let you know that even with the money obstacle you can still be successful making movies.

Funding is very complex when you are dealing with big budgets and investments. Since I'm talking about small budget films I can eliminate some of the most confusing issues, starting with the realities of life in the low budget filmmaking world:

1. No one, I repeat, no one is going to hand you $30 million to make your film. (Especially if you have no experience). Not going to happen.

2. No one is going to hand you $500,000, $250,000 or even $100,000 to make your first movie. Get the idea now?

3. In this day and age, unless you are related to one of the top five A list actors, have relatives in the business or working in the studio, finding money to make an independent low budget movie is almost impossible.

4. Never assume you have the best script ever written and there is no reason why they should not give you money. Scripts pile up on producers' desks written by people with writing experience in the business who cannot find funding. It is not an easy process.

Okay, so now you know nothing is free, this is the reality of the filmmaking life. You need to find a way to fund your film. It's not easy, but not impossible either. The one most important thing you have to learn and if you don't take anything else from this book, remember this:

You will be told by many, many people that they can help you, that they can get you funding. Your film script is wonderful; I can see it on the big screen. Blah, blah, blah, blah…bullshit.

From my personal experience, the majority of people in and surrounding this business are con artists, liars, and BS artists. This entire business is made up of illusions both in front of and behind the camera. People are looking for a way to make that quick buck. The promise of making you a star or marketing your name all over the world is what con artists use to lure you.

You NEVER give money upfront to ANYONE who promises you funding, NEVER. In fact, don't waste your time with more than one meeting with them. If they like your film, and have the funds, call them out and make them cough up some sort of seed money. Draw up a production agreement to make them become part of the film and make them walk the walk, not just talk the talk. You could literally waste weeks and months of your time with people who don't have a dime to their name but can talk a good game. Call them out as soon as they promise you something and when they don't produce what they promised then they are just full of crap. This will be 99 percent of the people you meet who call themselves producers.

TRUE STORY:

Let me share with you a few of our adventures about people who promised us funding. Just in the past two years alone, we have had three self-proclaimed executive producers willing to back our film projects.

First came Vancouver Jack (our nickname), a cocky Canadian producer with credits to his name. He told us, "Funding is not an issue, and have your attorney call me." Therefore, we set up a business plan, script, budget and shooting schedule for Canada. A couple of weeks of talks back and forth and it looked like this guy was interested in making a movie with us. Our attorney drew up a production agreement for the funds and ownership of the film and had been communicating with him all along. They had one last conference call set up for all of us to finalize the details. Our thought was we finally struck gold after months of talking to liars and BS artists. This guy had credits and access to funding so we thought we had a credible producer. Pop the cork, right? Wrong. Our attorney attempted the conference call at the specific time he requested. No answer, we tried again, no answer, an hour later, no answer, next day, no answer. We had invested a couple of weeks and valuable attorney time only to have this *putz* back out on us the day of the signing. This happens more often than you think.

That blunted our momentum and crushed our ego, but was hardly the worst song and dance we encountered. Soon after that, people heard what we went through and tried to help us out. We were connected to a woman who was the event organizer for former President Bush and had many connections to wealthy people. She had agreed to become our event planner, as well as our producer, and would commit to raising funds for our film. We agreed we would shoot our film at her clients' locations in exchange for funding as well as rooms and meals. Everything was progressing nicely. At our first meeting, she went out on a limb and promised us an easy fifty thousand dollars plus all the meals and rooms for the cast and crew. My bullshit radar goes off as soon as someone makes a statement like that. What she had promised us was worth at least seventy-five thousand dollars, plus she would add to that local product placement of another ten- or fifteen-thousand dollars. My brother and partner Tim thought she was a superstar, and

who know what they are doing. Always consult with your attorney before talking to people who may want to invest in your film.

What we like to do, and have been very successful with, is offer people from our group an active partner role in our film project. An active partner has a job on the movie and legally has no conflicts with the SEC. This could be your father, mother, brother, uncle or anyone who has some cash to help you through this process. Anyone who has been in this business will tell you there are no set rules on raising money and you do whatever works for you. That can mean bake sales, fundraising parties, bikini car washes, selling credits in your film…anything goes.

CROWD SOURCE FUNDING

Everyone today is talking about crowd source funding, like Indiegogo and Kickstarter, the two biggest. Personally, I don't know of one filmmaker who was able to raise enough money this way. In preparation for my last film, I decided to look at the numbers from crowd source funding sites and tabulated one thousand movies into the database and how many actually met their financing goal. I did allow some slack and, loosened up the numbers to see what the amount of success was. The numbers were shocking.

What I found was:

5 percent of films listed got 50 percent of what they asked for.
97 percent of all the films NEVER reached their goal at all.

To raise money this way you need to do a lot of work and you have to ask yourself if it's really worth the effort. We don't do crowd source funding because it takes a huge network of friends and family from around the country and hours and hours of time. I do not see crowd source funding working very well at all; in fact, it's almost a full-time job. With that being said, there have been new rules in place to help the small filmmakers attract qualified investors.

As of September 2013, filmmakers are now able to market their fundraising publicly, which means Tweeting, Facebooking, shouting from the rooftops, and taking billboards out on Sunset Boulevard. However, under Rule 506c (the rule allowing for general solicitation), filmmakers must make reasonable efforts to verify that their investors are accredited. The process of verifying an investor's accreditation depends on how an investor defines him/herself as accredited. It is a tedious process that involves investors providing filmmakers with two years of tax returns, or relevant bank statements/brokering statements/credit reports and more.

Investors may not be comfortable handing over this information to filmmakers directly, so the SEC has allowed regulated third parties to take on the essential due diligence. Investors may be happier being verified by a third party to prevent sensitive information being mismanaged by filmmakers. A regulated entity can be:

A registered investment advisor

A broker-dealer

An attorney

A CPA (certified public accountant)

Filmmakers also need to ensure that anyone participating in the fundraising does not fall under the BAD ACTOR provisions. This includes investors, investment advisors, producers or anyone else mentioned in the fundraising documentation. BAD ACTORS are individuals who have committed a crime, fraud, etc.

One new requirement filmmakers need to do in order to generally solicit is to file a Form D with the SEC, which most filmmakers do not do when soliciting funds privately. This form lets the SEC know you are raising money using an exemption. Under today's law if you are using general solicitation, Form D needs to be filed 15 days after the first investment is made.

Under future proposed rules, the form needs to be filed 3 times:

15 days before you use the 506c exemption

15 days after the first investment is made

30 days following the termination of an offering

If filmmakers do not follow the proposed rules, they could lose their fundraising exemption, which can give the investors the Right of Rescission (the right to get their money back), or land themselves in jail. Should the SEC investigate the offering, or legal action is taken by investors in the film, the burden will be on the filmmaker to prove the fundraising has been done in compliance with the rules.

While new laws definitely help indie filmmakers solicit investors for their films, many hidden rules still must be followed. Again, my advice is to have your attorney help you get on the proper path to fundraising.

FILM SPONSORS AND PRODUCT PLACEMENT

Something we learned early on, and essential for our films, is to get sponsors and product placement. At first, it was difficult to attract people to become sponsors in a local film that may or may not be shown anywhere. Couple that with the fact that every dipshit with a camcorder making a zombie movie was hitting up the local businesses for money and you have a toxic situation. Since we had no track record at all on our first movie, we had a dilemma. No one is going to give you product or money with nothing to show in return. It got easier and easier as we began to sell our films. We guesstimate we saved a couple thousand dollars per shoot by getting small local companies to donate products we could include in the shot including:

Coffee and teas
Liquor
Pizza
Sneakers
Sweatshirts
Energy drinks
Muffins
Breakfast food

This is just a partial list of some of the companies willing to help you. You have to remember, product placement is a two-way street. Your film has to get seen if you're asking them for product. As I said far too many times, we have approached local merchants to get their product in our films only to find out that some of the other local yahoo filmmakers already got free product from them and never finished their movie. I can honestly say we have encountered this at least 80 percent of the time in our market. Even though we have a track record of selling movies, businesses continue rejecting the idea entirely. What ends up happening is that you get lumped into the category of deadbeat filmmakers because a few wannabes spoil the entire process.

Distance yourself from the wannabe or the bottom feeders, as I call them. The last thing you need is to be compared to someone who never finished a movie, yet took their product. Local businesses are putting trust in you and your film, so it has to work for them as well as you. You have to make sure your film gets some sort of exposure, not just You Tube, local distribution on cable TV or the local art house theater;

they have to get exposure for the products they give to you. You will always see local filmmakers go out and talk to the local beer companies, the local restaurants about putting products in their movies, but 99.9 percent of those movies never leave their living rooms, if they get done at all. That is a losing situation for the sponsor. Don't be like them.

YOUR SCRIPT

What is your script about?

Is the story unique?

Has it been done one trillion times?

Will it be attractive to a buyer?

Will it put an audience in the seats?

As an independent filmmaker, you need to do research and find these things out. Is there audience interest in your genre?

NOTE: A point to remember is that, pretty much, everything has been done. What will make your story different, sellable? Outline a bunch of ideas and notes:

Are these good stories?

Can you visualize them?

Can you get them from paper to the screen?

Are you being realistic?

Can you shoot this small budget?

One of the biggest mistakes filmmakers make is biting off more than they can chew. With a $20,000 budget, you are not going to get that helicopter shot you wanted, (helicopters cost about $1,000 an hour.) Be realistic with yourself. Think about what you have access to in the here and now. Do you have a relative's house? Basement? The woods or garage? Then write your script accordingly.

Script format is also important; you want this to be taken seriously. You can find many great script-formatting programs out there, don't spend too much money. Celtic is a free program that is a favorite of indie filmmakers. It's a powerful free program that will format your script. I suggest you get your idea into Celtic.

NOTE: Always be open-minded while inviting criticism of your story and be prepared for the director to throw away 30 percent of what you wrote.

I make this a point to writers and filmmakers in my classes, especially when I taught at the International Screenwriters Conference in L.A. In every instance, you could see their jaws drop to the floor; they could not comprehend that their script would be changed at all.

The truth is the script is just a guideline. In every case the director (if not you) will come across a situation that has to be changed, be it a location, a character action or a line in the script. You will never, never shoot by the script in its entirety without changing it. You can always count on changes to the script on location. Be prepared, and bring a printer and extra paper on location.

KNOWLEDGE OF THE BUSINESS

Without a doubt in our world, the more you know the easier it will be to do.

Knowledge is power. The fact you're reading this book says you strive for excellence. You are the kind of person who wants to be successful. You have the zest to learn more about this business; experience brings you that knowledge. In my case, thirty years as a professional, shooting, directing, editing, and producing, I can honestly say I've seen it all in this business. I feel the knowledge I have accrued should be passed on to others so they may limit their mistakes. The only way to learn is by doing. If you want to make movies the only way to learn is by making movies.

Before you decide to go to film school and get bombarded by film theory taught by some professor who has never walked on to a film set, get some real world experience. In fact, I can promise you one thing: Everything you learn in the film class you can throw out the window once you walk onto your movie set.

One particular problem motivated me to write this book. Book theory has nothing to do with what happens on a film shoot. Once I got into the real production world everything I was taught in the classroom was useless. You learn by doing.

BUDGET

Okay, so you're reading this book, you know you can make a movie. You disagree with some of the things I have said, but you are taking valuable notes. You have confidence your script is good and lined up a few local businesses willing to work with you. You have the tenacity of a pit bull and a solid support structure.

Only question now is how much money do you have? I have always said if I were a different type of artist, a painter or sculptor, I would only need some clay and canvases and I can start making art. Being a filmmaker takes a bit more…okay, a lot more money. I always say, "It takes money to make a movie and it takes money to sell a movie."

However, all is not lost, it still can be done. Let's assume you did a fundraising campaign and let's look at some of the options you took advantage of.

NOTE: Always remember that unless you are working in the Hollywood studio system there are no rules or set ways to raise money, it's all up to you. So let's say you get a few things working for you.

So, you had a cool fundraising bash.
Have some family and friends that will kick in.

Went to sponsors to find products for your film.

Sold some partnerships in your movie.

Put up a page for crowd source funding.

You tried all these things and after all that, you only raised $9000…that's it. But that's $9,000 more than you had when you started. Fundraising is a battle; a war you never stop.

I can tell you that one of our films was made for just about eleven thousand dollars. I killed myself to get it finished, developed an ulcer, but got it done. Not only was it one of the 2 percent completed, it secured one of our worldwide distribution deals for ten years. So yes, you can do it on a micro budget. Here are a few things you can do:

Find qualified people willing to work cheaply enough for food expenses and for a percentage of the movie or the back end.

Offer your cast and crew a one-time stipend for the entire film. That payment covers some of their expenses. You also pay for their food and accommodations and give them percentage of the film (back end).

You use sponsors to offset your food costs, such as bagels, breakfast sandwiches subs, pizzas, calzones…are all great.

Develop a menu around your sponsored food and this will really help you save money feeding the cast and crew.

You will have to have some funds to pay your cast and crew; the most important thing is to make sure everyone is paid before you. Keep the cast and crew happy by giving them money up front, before you get paid anything.

If you have family, friends and crew members who can make big salads and help prepare meals you are one up on the food costs. You will have to be very creative.

NOTE: Food and accommodations are the biggest cost for small indie film when shooting on location. You must feed the cast and crew three meals a day. Don't skip or skimp on meals. Make sure you feed them well.

NOTE: Never, never serve pasta or carbohydrates for lunch.

We did this on our first film only to have our cast and crew sugar crash by 3 p.m. Carbohydrates turn to sugars quickly. Salads, wraps, and fruits are all good to serve. Pizza for lunch will certainly slow down your production.

Keep a detailed log of the food money spent.

Be sure you don't give into whimsical wants and requests. This business breeds egos, even in the low budget world. Actors will ask for certain things like fruity water, sweets, or sodas. Filmmakers don't entertain divas. Everyone gets treated the same with no special treatment or you will blow through your cash faster than you are ready for.

TRUE STORY:

On our first film, we brought on a wonderful woman who could cook like no one else. We knew this task would be daunting so we decided to get her some help in the form of a PA. While we trusted our craft services mom, we had no idea if the PA was up to the task. We let our craft services mom run the show. After a couple of days, we noticed multiple trips being made to the local supermarket for gallons of soda. Since we were so busy, we didn't think much of it. The next day we noticed boxes full of water and soda being unloaded again by the PA. I asked our craft services mom what was going on with all the soda and water? She was unsure because it wasn't anything she needed. The next day we decided to look into our food budget and went through all the receipts. We had gone through our entire food budget in the first five days of shooting. We still had five more days on location. I was ballistic, since I was funding this film myself. Turns out the PA was helping other crew members store away soda and munchies in their rooms for after the shoot. By the time our partner Tim had the chance to oversee their screw-ups it cost me another $1,500 to restock our supplies, largely because we went with bottled water, and let the cast and crew dictate their needs. A person on the inside got them what they wanted.

That never happened to us again. On the next films we developed a menu, supplies were listed and everyone got what we had to give. Special treats were outlawed unless we all got them. Of course, as the director I made sure the food budget always had money for ice cream with my PAs after each shoot. That's a perk of being the director.

LEGAL

You know I had to get there at some point—the legalities of making a movie. Artists and lawyers are like oil and water. We will always need them. Fortunately, for us, our attorney

Jim Pross has become a friend; we have him make an appearance in all our films. That being said, the legal aspect of filmmaking will need the attention of a smart attorney. Whether optioning a script, copyrighting documents, legal release forms or talking to potential investors, you will need legal help. Make sure you are prepared for this. Cast release forms, location release forms and crew deal memos will be needed for each and every person involved with the production.

NOTE: One of the most important documents you will need is production insurance. Odds are you may not need your attorney for this; however, it would be smart to run any type of insurance document by him/her. Production insurance is needed for any legitimate production to cover the location and business owner and yourself. Liability will cover any injuries that may occur to another person on the set. The minimum liability for production insurances, as of this writing, is one million dollars. Some public locations and towns may require up to two million dollars to allow shooting on public property. Shop around and make sure you have production insurance; if not, you can and will be held liable as well as everyone associated with your film. Dozens of production insurance companies are online. The good news is that a temporary production insurance binder is fairly inexpensive, for example, a policy for two or three weeks will cost you around $600, that's if your film has no stunts or car chases. You will find the quote skyrocketing to a couple thousand dollars or more if you add in fight scenes and action sequences.

Again, you should always run these legal documents by your attorney.

Another good thing is you won't need your attorney services until the end of your film, when you begin to shop your film around to distributors. Make sure you have some sort of budget for your attorney to help you with the legal aspects of filmmaking.

PRE-PRODUCTION

Okay, let's see, you have all your ducks in a row, everything finally lined up. You have your best friend as your partner, you feel ready to go. Now it's time to put this project together. Who is helping you make your movie?

Producers

Camera operator

Assistant directors

Soundman or woman

Make up

Production assistants

Script supervisor
It's time to get everyone in one room; easy, right? Hardly. In fact, almost impossible thanks to day jobs, classes, kids...there is always a reason why people cannot make a meeting.

NOTE: We have had so many meetings that only half the people showed up and meetings became a waste of time. We began to test the dedication of our crew members by offering a free breakfast meeting Sunday morning at 8 a.m.; after all, you will be shooting early. Can your people be up at 6 a.m.? Are they truly committed to the film? Have a Saturday or Sunday crew meeting at 8 a.m. and you'll soon see who's with you and who you need to replace.

Pre-production: start assigning jobs to crew

Working out shoot dates

Finding locations

Casting for parts

Buying/Renting equipment

Getting insurance

Breaking down the script

Rewriting the script

Planning food menus

Planning transportation

Planning rooms and travel

These are all elements of the pre-production process. Each specific task will be delegated to one person that has the skills to do that job.

You will set up:
Weekly meetings

'To do' deadlines

Problem-solving tasks

Use your calendar with weekly meetings to set up dates of when things are to be done.

Keep open discussions with people. Should they run into problems be ready to assign them help or help them yourself.

Do not assume that just because you delegated assignments at the first meeting that they are being done…always follow up on it midweek with an email to get an update status. If something falls through the crack (and it always does), you need to address it at your next meeting.

Have a pre-production checklist.

Be organized. You need to have a smooth pre-production; otherwise production will be chaos.

Keep a binder for all your paperwork. I have a huge three ring binder I call the 'shoot bible' and I use this same binder for each film. I keep in it EVERYTHING:

All release forms

All insurance documents

Scheduling info

Cast and crew phone numbers

The script

Emergency phone numbers

Lawyer's phone number

All letters and emails from important people and distributors

At the beginning of each film, I hand the shoot bible to the second AD. Second ADs are required to babysit the shoot bible during the duration of the film. They are responsible for keeping it up to date and filing away all the necessary forms. Set up your shoot during production while information is being created. It is crucial to do this from the start.

CHAPTER 3

CASTING

Casting is very important, and you need to able to evaluate talent quickly. The process involves hiring the best actors and actresses you can find. Don't let it become a popularity contest by picking the most popular or best-looking people. Make sure you choose the most talented people available. You will find most résumés chock full of past experiences and you will also find some full of useless information.

You need to meet the cast in person. Today, video auditions are very popular, but they show no commitment to your film. Let the actors drive to you and wait in line. Make them invest the time in your film. You need to see what kind of dedication they truly have.

TRUE STORY:

We went the traditional route casting our films for the first two features. We noticed people were getting lazy or we were not getting the message. Actors started asking us to look at their reel online. During our casting, we had almost half the people intending to submit an online audition. Our casting director said this is the wave of the future. Our producers disagreed and decided you get in your car, drive to our casting call, and meet us personally or you are not in our film. We decided to stick to this decision; after all, you have to put some skin in the game. What we found out is that other filmmakers in our area were letting people audition online. All those films were amateur projects that will never get sold anyway. That was fine for them; however, we wanted them to physically come to the audition. We ruffled some feathers and pissed off a few of the so-called filmmakers because they had their favorites they wanted in our films and we said, "Then make the audition." We could care less what other filmmakers had to say and we stuck to our guns. We eventually sold the movie using only people who attended our auditions. The other filmmakers are still mad at us for not giving into their ways and considering their favorites. I have a formula for success, and they still have not sold a film. Stick to your decisions, once you make a rule stay with it. For us, video auditions were not an option.

The best way to organize your casting is to have local casting director help; someone who knows all the local and regional talent. Someone who can circulate announcements as to what you need. Casting directors usually have a good feel of what talent is in the area. I would strongly urge you to bring in someone with casting knowledge who will make the casting process so much easier on you. Casting can be a very confusing process if not done properly.

TRUE STORY:

I can remember casting for our first feature film in a small office of a renovated mill with long hallways and high ceilings, like something right out of a scary movie. We decided to do a two-day casting. We wondered how many people could be there on a two-day casting. We had our core group at the head tables and our casting director would read the lines with them. We had two production assistants handing out sides (sides are just a couple of pages of the script you think are crucial to see if they can play that character). The casting had a steady flow of potential actors and actresses, all of them believing they had what it took to be in our movie. We easily cruised through the morning session. We had people scheduled about ten minutes apart and it was somewhat organized. We broke for lunch at a little deli across the street. All of us evaluated the people we saw, not mentioning how smooth it went…that would have been a curse. After lunch, when we got back to the office, we were shocked; seventy-five to one hundred people lined the hallway, waiting for the afternoon session. We were overwhelmed. More were coming in the door. We had issued an open casting call, or cattle call, for the afternoon, and we really believed we wouldn't see that many people in the afternoon session. Now, chaos beckoned. Instead of spacing people every ten minutes we had people reading back to back. Although it was really crazy, reads went really well. We found that to have an organized casting it is best to make time slots available and not to have an open casting call. The best way to stay organized is by scheduling a person every five or ten minutes.

Avoid an open casting call, or cattle call, because you may get bum-rushed by many people and it's very, very chaotic.

The actual casting setup is quite easy. Have one or two actors or actresses read two or three parts during the audition. Have a camcorder set up; shoot all the performances, no matter how good or how bad…get them on tape or SD card.

NOTE: Be very nice to the actors and thank them for their read. Always thank them for their time and participating in the casting. You never know when you may need them for your next project.

I have seen directors ridicule people in an audition only to find them in the lead role on a bigger project. There is a very old saying in Hollywood: "Be kind to those you meet on the way up because you may be seeing them again on your way down."

A well-organized casting will give you the chance to work with a big talent pool. Save all their information, your actors and actresses will have professional headshots and, hopefully, a well done resume to hand to your people…keep them. The point here is if they don't fit in this movie project they may be right for your next project. Keep lists of each cast member and contact information.

EVALUATING TALENT

During the casting process, I use a three star system:

- One star actor or actress is a bit weak

- Two stars is an average actor/actress

- Three stars on the page means they're very talented

Once they get three stars, we want to see them again, obviously. You only want to bring aboard a three-star actor/actress. However, sometimes an actor or actress is not always available for your shoot date. Always have a list on hand in your shoot bible of potential backups. You never know when you will need to go to that list in the event your first choice is unavailable.

Study the video of the casting. I post it online and have my core group pick their favorites. I like feedback from all different perspectives. On our crew, for instance, the DP (director of photography) may see something in the way they walk or the make-up supervisor may catch something about their complexion or what they shouldn't wear. Use your team's eyes and experience to get feedback and data. Remember this is a team sport; you cannot make a movie alone. Study, study, study the video to listen to their delivery. Is there passion in their voice? Are they just reading? These are the people on your frontline; choose the best you can find from your casting. There is always the possibility you may need to do a second casting. It does happen. You can never know how everyone will work together once the hot lights hit them. All you can do is be prepared to guide them through the filmmaking process. Use encouragement as much as possible and be prepared to be fair, yet stern, to get your message across.

LOCATIONS

Cameras once were big and bulky and lights weighed as much as a Volkswagen. In those days, most of the productions were shot in a soundstage. Moving that equipment around was not an option. Soundstages are still around today, especially for the production of TV shows and sitcoms; however, most films today are shot on location. With the exception of the green screen shots for CGI work, most movies want real locations. The filmmaker, working on a tight budget, really can't afford the hourly rental rates a soundstage charges. Shooting on location is much more cost efficient than creating an entire living room or bedroom set. If you watch our films, you will notice our low budget productions always have enticing visual value. We always find locations never seen in micro/low budget movies. This makes our films look much more like large budget productions, thus making them more attractive to potential distributors. Locations like:

Churches

Bars and restaurants

Ferryboats

Police stations

Forts

Diners

Stables

These are all locations that low budget filmmakers usually can't get. We pride ourselves in the fact we secure these types of locations. It certainly makes a difference to the credibility of your film.

Shooting at some locations can be very tricky and anytime you want to shoot on location, you're going to need to have insurance. Business locations will ask you for proof of insurance to shoot in their establishment. The best way to make your low budget film more commercial and give it credibility is to always shoot in a real location. It can't hurt to offer the owner an extra role in the film as a perk. Be as realistic with your script as you can. For example, if your script calls for a police station, then get a real police station. You may have to shoot that scene at three o'clock in the morning, but you will be glad you did. It will add reality to your script. Make sure you have secured permission to shoot on the premises and always get a signed location release, as I spoke about previously.

TRUE STORY:

I can tell you early in my career about a situation we had shooting in a local restaurant. The owner had invited friends to come in and sit in as extras in the restaurant while we did the shoot and he spared no expense. Full course plates sat on every table the set up looked amazing. We had done a few walk-throughs, and I wanted to change the angle of the shot. The shot was great; we had a nice family in the foreground and a good-looking middle-age couple in the background, the family was in focus and the couple in the background was in soft focus. We decided to rack focus and dolly at the same time. Rack focusing is moving focusing from one object to the other and changing the focus from background to foreground or vice versa. We did four or five takes of that and the owner was very happy with what he saw.

After we broke down the owner fed all the crew from that massive pile of food left over in the kitchen. We had our own feast. A bit later, after stuffing ourselves, we were loading our equipment in the van and just about to leave when I realized I forgot to get the owner's signature on a release form. The release form gave us permission to shoot in his restaurant and vouched for the extras in the shots. Legally the release form shifted the responsibility of the extras in his establishment to him. He has given us permission to shoot all of them in his restaurant. We also made sure he made that announcement live before we stared shooting. Since all of them were friends or family, he would vouch for them.

It was about a week later when I got a call from the restaurant owner. I had sent him a copy of the raw footage to look at. He wanted to have a small screening with the people who were there that night. He said, "It was wonderful." He told me the footage looked great. However, there was one exception, a problem. He totally overlooked this that night due to his hectic schedule. He told me a golfing friend, one of the good-looking couple behind the family, didn't think he would be visible on camera but when they viewed the footage that night he was plainly visible. The couple was obviously a bit hammered not to realize they were in the shot. The man was at the table with a woman who was not his wife. Unfortunately, or idiotically enough, he had brought his wife to the screening of the raw footage. The camera shows him and his mistress/girlfriend sitting at the table eating and drinking. I can only imagine what that ride home was like. What saved us from any kind of embarrassment or having to re-shoot was getting the owner to sign the release form giving us permission to shoot his establishment and patrons that night. He had even made an announcement.

The message here is to make sure you have a signed location form from every location you shoot.

STORYBOARDS

Hollywood makes a big deal out of having storyboards done. No doubt they spend more on storyboards than we spend on our entire films. The truth about storyboards is they are a tool, like anything else. They help the director convey his vision to the cast and crew.

The market offers some very good storyboard software programs. One of our sponsors, the people at Storyboard Quick, has an easy-to-use software that will do everything you need. Digital storyboards look great. If you cannot afford storyboard software, the best tried-and-true way of doing storyboards is just having them hand drawn by someone who can draw.

TRUE STORY:

I was so excited to have the perfect storyboards done for our first film that I decided to hand draw each scene onto large index cards. Thinking this will help the DP, cast and crew, I spent countless hours getting these scenes drawn. When I think back on how much time it actually took, I cringe. What ends up happening is you place the index cards in one of your transport vehicles, move a few loads of equipment in and out and they end up scattered all over the floor of the van.

My advice is if you truly want impressive storyboards have an artist draw them for you. An artist can make them quicker and save you hours and hours of time. You can get caught up in drawing storyboards and digital storyboards are no different. Once I found software that would do my storyboards on my iPad, I found myself again spending hours creating them. Keep your storyboards simple, or have someone who can draw quickly create them for you. They may be fun to do, but you can waste valuable time doing them.

If you have the time to learn the software that's fine, but if you're as impatient as I am, nothing is wrong with hand-drawing a few scenes of the movie or having someone else draw them. This software has a big learning curve. Scenes for your storyboard could be as complex as comic books or as simple as symbols drawn on a napkin. Don't get too hung up on the storyboard, you have far more important things to worry about. Convey your vision with storyboards. If you do decide to go full speed ahead, the one thing you should have is a sharp multi-frame storyboard. This needs to be done if you have many people and businesses involved.

Storyboards are a very cool sales and presentation tool to help outsiders visualize what you trying to do. For the iPad users, I use a sharp storyboard app called Storyboards 3-D. On our film, *Dark Minds,* I actually had fun making storyboards. Storyboards 3-D is very easy to use. If you have an iPad, that is maybe something to look at.

EQUIPMENT

Here is the trillion-dollar question: What type of equipment do I use to shoot my movie? There was a time not that long ago when you had one option, 16mm film or 35mm film or even Super 8mm film for that matter. Having lived and worked through the analog to digital transition from film to HD, I know the different schools of thought. I do like the look of full HD at 24fps.

I believe it doesn't have the look and movement of motion picture film. I don't believe it ever will.

Film has a more organic feel and depth. I call it personality. That being said, I am assuming most people reading this book are working in the digital environment.

It's impossible to justify shooting film unless you have a huge budget.

Film cameras are still used to shoot feature films, commercial and television shows. HD (high definition) is making inroads but has a way to go before it will become a popular format for the big-budget Hollywood production.

Companies like Red, Sony and Arri are perfecting HD cinema cameras that look amazing.

If you are shooting in film, then you are quite adventurous. I would love to hear more about your project. Shooting film comes with a series of rules and procedures. The most important thing you will need to know is that syncing audio on film cameras is an art form. Crystal sync controlled cameras need to be operated by people who know what they are doing. Some great 16mm sync cameras are lying around if you are shooting on 16mm. One camera to look at, the Cinema Products VP-16, a crystal sync camera that makes it easy to sync up your audio with your video. These were workhorses in their day and were built like a tank. They were primarily used to shoot news footage, but that's another book entirely. Shooting film is a different world. For this book, I will concentrate on the digital format. Questions you will need to ask yourself:

What do I shoot with?

What format do I use?

What cameras are best?

I am asked this question every time I meet aspiring filmmakers. I usually surprise them when I give them the same answer, "Use what you have." The majority of the time they expect me to rattle off three or four high-end cameras they need to shoot with. In truth, you don't need them.

Nothing drives me more insane than some pampered rich kid getting a Canon 5D camera for his birthday just because he thinks shooting film may be fun. His parents drop four grand on a 5D kit to let precious little Johnny play director. What usually happens is little Johnny gets bored and the camera sits on a shelf after a couple uses.

Hundreds of potential filmmakers want to work their butts off but can't afford the gear. That is why I say, "Use what you have."

You can always find people in your own town who have access to money and equipment. To me that doesn't mean they have the talent or ambition. I have a saying in this business when that subject comes up, and it comes up often:

"There are those with talent and no money and then there are those with money and no talent."

If you have no gear to use, borrow gear from your friends or family members. Someone will have a HD camera you can use. Ask around to see who has gear that is not being used. Maybe they would be willing to shoot your film in exchange for credits or even a percentage of your movie. If you cannot overcome this first little hurdle then you certainly will not be able to think outside the box enough to get a film made.

NOTE: I'm not a big fan of people who tell me you need a certain type of gear; that this is what everyone is using, etc. We shot our first short film with a consumer hi 8mm camera. At the time they looked great. It's not the gear you use; it's how you use it. In the past couple of years, I have seen some iPhone short films that were as good as any high end HD camera. The camera is a tool; a brush for you to paint with. We shot two of our features with cameras not meant for filmmaking. Don't listen to people.

Equipment gets outdated every couple of months. I strongly discourage people from going out and spending thousands of dollars on equipment that will be obsolete in six months. Keep it simple:

List all the gear you have

Find out what gear is available for you to borrow

Find people who have gear and want to be on your crew

Pull it all together and know what gear you have to shoot your movie, then research and practice with the gear you have.

Know what the current formats and codecs are. Know how you will be able to edit them and if your editor is up to date. Today, you will need to study formats you should shoot in, such as tape-based HDV camcorders, SD card HD cameras and DSLR cameras. Look into the workflow and how easy or difficult they are to edit.

SD card based cameras are the most popular today, although many people shoot tape based HD like HDV and DVC Pro. One of my favorite little HDV cameras is the Vixia HV 30, a large sensor single chip HDV camera that shoots amazing footage in 30p and 24p. When color corrected, it can still compete with higher end HD cameras.

When shooting HD feature films you have two options, the consumer or the professional grade camera. If you have a lot of money, obviously, go with the professional gear. Again, don't let anyone tell you that you can't shoot a movie on a consumer camera. HD cameras today are quite good; while it's not easy to make a feature film on a consumer-based camera, you will need to put in extra work. We did it with the HV 30s on our film, *Back to the Beyond.*

TRUE STORY:

During the pre-production process for *Back to the Beyond,* we tried several cameras because we had a tiny budget and we had no money to rent gear at all. DSLRs were not quite ready for features and still expensive. We had access to the Panasonic AG-DVX 100Bs, or we could go with the two

Canon HV30. Since I had tons of extra batteries and gear for the HV30s, I decided to go with the HV30 and shoot in 24p, even though I knew the editing process would be hell. These cameras do not shoot native 24p, which means all the footage had to be transferred and transcoded. They also shoot in what is called a 1080i wrapper. This means all the footage has to be unwrapped in a program and digitally converted to get to the actual 24fps video. The technical term is removing the pull down. This is on top of being transcoded. It is like peeling away the coconut shell to get to the milk. This all has to be done before it can be brought into Final Cut Pro.

The process took weeks just to get the footage in the editor but once I looked at the shots, I had no regrets. When I compared the footage from the Panasonic to the Canon HV30 the HV30 blew it away. We shot the entire film on two HV 30s, edited 24p on Final Cut Pro. The film was sold to Maxim Films International.

It was an editing nightmare but it did get done. You also have to remember that consumer cameras have a limited light range. Some don't have microphone inputs and are extremely limited in dark scenes. The point here is: use what you have. Even though we shot our film *Back to Beyond* with Canon HV 30s, it became a worldwide-distributed feature film.

DSLRs are the new wave for indie filmmakers. They have light bodies, large sensors and interchangeable lenses; you really have to think hard about what you will need before shooting with a DSLR. Make sure you do research before using a DSLR.

NOTE: DSLRs were not designed to shoot movies, especially feature films. They are not ergonomically correct and you need all kinds of camera mounts to get a customized, comfortable fit. DSLR shooting takes a ton of patience, changing lenses takes a long time and focus is difficult when shooting on dark sets. If you already own a DSLR then, by all means, use what you have and do the best you can with it. Some great inexpensive Canon DSLRs on the market look great. Canons also have a microphone input as well as 24p. While the indie filmmaker is just getting used to shooting 1080p with DSLRs and video cameras, the market seems to be changing. The new highly touted format for independent filmmakers and distributors is 4K which has a much better film look but costs much more money. I have talked to our distributors who say 4K will be the new acquisition format soon but for now full HD 1920 x 1080 is a great shooting resolution. When you consider only a few years ago that production was done in a 720 SD format, this is certainly a step up. Many, if not most, indies shoot in 1080p. However, that's changing fast because of the bigger chips and the call for 2K and 4K resolutions; 2K being slightly larger than 1920 x 1080 and the 4K resolution looks closer to 35mm film.

Don't concern yourself over shooting 2K or 4K. If you can shoot in 1080p you're fine. You will find editing 1080p is quite easy. It's a technical challenge when you start shooting and talking about working with 2K or 4K formats. You are looking at cameras that need highly skilled camera operators, as well as specific software and huge amounts of storage with super fast processors. Right now, indies are content shooting 1080p and distributors are still acquiring films in that format. 1080p right now is probably the easiest format to shoot in. So, let's recap:

Shoot with what you have.

Make sure you have 1080p at least 24 frames a second.

30 frames per second is also preferred by some filmmakers.

Don't go out and buy gear if you have access to it.

Don't get caught up in the hype of 2K or 4K.

Don't watch what others are doing or shooting, stay focused on you.

Get your film done. That is the key here; remember to use what you have and make it as good as you can. Until we see the distributors demanding to have films shot in 2K or 4K, 1080p is the easiest to edit and work.

LIGHTING

The one area indie films really lack is great lighting. I have always considered lighting to be my strength; in fact, I took the Arri lighting certification classes a few years back and found them to be very interesting. I realized that even after lighting for thirty years, I needed to know more. When creating the look and mood for motion pictures, lighting is a specialty and makes all the difference in the production value of your project. Lighting sets creates the overall feeling of the film.

TRUE STORY:

When you have a film screened by distributors, they will evaluate your film for production value. Some will use a number or letter system and some just use their eye to determine if your film has any production value at all. Many factors go into determining a film's production value. The three biggest factors are:

Camerawork

Lighting

Sound

We have all watched indie films that lack one, two or all three of these elements. A true commercial film will be solid in all three. Production value is crucial when you are talking about your film being released in a catalogue of motion pictures that cost, literally, fifty to one hundred times more to produce. Fair or not, audiences today are watching two hundred million dollar films, then they rent your little film the next day. They don't know or care what your film costs to make; they only know your sound is not like the monster budget film they just rented, or that your lighting was off. All they see is your film did not look like the Universal Studios or Lions Gate release. It is important that you work hard to put some production value into your feature film. This all starts with being very meticulous with your sound, lighting, and camerawork.

Production lighting is rated on a Kelvin scale:

Blue Sky outside = 10,000K

Overcast outside = 7,000K

Daylight/sunlight = 5,600K

Fluorescent lights = 4,300K

Household bulbs = 2,700K

Candlelight = 1,800K

Working with different lights and color temperatures is another skill acquired. The idea of lighting is to know what color temperature you are working in so you can balance your camera for that lighting.

Professional lights are very costly. I have seen instances where low budget filmmakers used work lights to light a scene. This is not something you should do. If you have no background in lighting then you need to read up as much as you can. The new generation of filmmakers has a new friend as far as lighting goes in CFL lights. When your budget does not allow you to purchase or rent professional lights, take a quick trip to Home Depot and you will find many different types of CFL bulbs. For the consumer they are called soft white or cool white bulbs. Read the label and you will see different lighting temperatures you can purchase cheaply. Same for CFL lighting kits which are much more costly. Two general rules for lighting will always apply:

Indoor lighting bulbs, lamps etc. are always rated at 3,200K.

Outdoor lighting, sunlight, noon sun is always rated at 5,600K.

You should be able to purchase 3,200K CFL bulbs to shoot indoors.

Lighting is a skill, so you need to practice as much as possible. To get good lighting you will need someone with some lighting experience. Usually your DP and AC will have a background in lighting and can get the look you need.

I'm sure you've seen some low budget films with no light, too much light or lighting that's really bad. Harsh lighting on the characters is bad production value. You don't want your scenes to look like old home movies. Some of the best people with lighting chops are photographers. If you're unsure about lighting, you have to dive in head first on lighting research. Try to find some good resource books on basic lighting principles. Make sure your scenes are lit well.

We have always used different type of lights on our shoots. At one point, when shooting music video, we even purchased work lights, using a diffusion gel in front of the lamps to smooth out the light, and they looked great. The idea is to make sure you have enough light. You will find purchasing a diffusion kit for your lights will also give you flexibility and control over the light. We like B&H Photo and Video for this kind of purchase. There you will find some of the more popular diffusion sheets to help you balance the room light. Lee and Rosco are the most popular.

NOTE: Never shoot a scene without lights. That will be the first tip off to potential buyers that your film has no production value. Excellent lighting will look natural, not too dark or too harsh. Bring in someone like a photographer, someone who knows lighting setups to help you with your film. Lighting sets today really has not changed that much in fifty years or more. Many soundstages still use the big, hot, bulky quartz lights and halogen light kits. There has been some new technology in the past ten years with the creation of LED and CFL lighting kits. The daylight balanced fluorescent lighting kits make a set much, much cooler, they are lightweight and easy to set up, as well as very cost-effective. LED and CFL kits give off a really soft light and a smooth look for your film. Assuming you are on a tight budget, you can still find halogen lights on eBay. Many old TV light kits are floating around that will make your DP happy.

Do a search online for daylight balanced CFL bulbs because they are an inexpensive light and you can build your own small kit with a few bulbs, receptacles, and aluminum reflectors purchased from your local hardware store. Another excellent source of soft light would be to purchase a bunch of white China balls to drop over your CFL bulbs.

China balls are great soft lighting for people sitting at a table or accent lighting on plants, room corners, etc., and very, very inexpensive.

China balls are also a very good source of lighting on a budget. They are easy to use, stay cool, and are lightweight enough to carry around. Lighting is very important. If you have to, purchase a small CFL lighting kit or old video light kit on eBay. The thing to remember with older halogen or quartz bulbs is they are quite expensive, very hot and don't have a long life.

No matter what type of light you use, I highly recommend you view many tutorials on setting up a one, two, and three point lighting scheme. You will need to know the basics to get started. Again, your film will be critiqued on its production value. Lighting is a major part of that. Lighting, sound and camerawork all factor into the production value equation.

AUDIO RECORDING

The biggest killer and I mean the BIGGEST KILLER of all indie films is bad audio and audio editing. Yes, camerawork, lighting, actors, and script all factor into a movies success but bad audio will sink your film faster than all other production elements.

Bad audio means no distribution deal.

I learned early that I would dedicate a huge amount of audio editing, audio clean up, and audio re-creation on my films.

TRUE STORY:

In post-production of our first feature film, I knew the proper way to handle the audio was to discard the location audio completely and have the actors come back into the studio and lay down their exact lines under controlled conditions. This is known as ADR (automatic dialogue recording or replacement). This is how Hollywood filmmakers do it. Essentially, they start with just a picture and a silent movie and re-create the dialogue, sound effects and room noises. I was very familiar with the process.

The catch? Money. It takes a couple of months and thousands of dollars to have the actors return to read all their lines. While ADR is a way of life in big budget films, I could not justify or afford to do ADR on this low budget project. With that in mind, we were very careful as to how we recorded our audio. We always have three or four different recorders on location running at the same.

We still use that same concept today. ADR is not a low budget filmmaker's friend so you really need to concentrate on getting the best possible audio you can on location.

I cannot stress enough, recording great audio is not just important, it is necessary. Get a great shotgun microphone like a Sennheiser or AKG shotgun. With proper placement and a good operator a shotgun microphone will give you quality, useable audio for your film's dialogue. You will still need to do some audio editing and tweaking in post-production. It is imperative to always have two people listening to your audio on location beside yourself.

NOTE: Have at least two sets of headsets on location with two people monitoring audio.

TRUE STORY:

Audio will always be the thing that slips through the cracks. On *Dark Minds*, we set up all the proper checkpoints to make sure the audio was being monitored, both off the camera and from the mic itself. What we had failed to do is to listen to the room in total silence. In each office, we found ourselves with a different florescent hum. We were using high-end sound dampening headsets. While they are great for isolation, they isolate everything. Throughout the entire movie in every office we shot, we had this low hum we did not hear on the set. It's very frustrating to have almost perfect audio.

All is not lost however. Check out a great, and I mean great, noise reduction software called Soundsoap Pro. Soundsoap has a small learning curve. Once you have it mastered, you will be amazed at how quickly and cleanly you can take out hums and unwanted noises in your dialogue tracks. They also make a condensed version called Soundsoap 2. You will be very happy you made that investment. This little piece of software will allow you to strip down the dialogue track and scrub it clean. You can then lay it back down and sync it back up to your characters. To the low budget indie, that's as close to ADR as you can get without spending the money.

Be sure to have another set of ears on headsets for something you may miss. Audio is a specialty so find someone who has some experience and someone who works with audio. I give the soundman or woman *carte blanche* to cut a take anytime during filming on my shoots. The last thing you want is to watch your dailies and hear some motorcycle or truck that makes your audio unusable. Make sure you give your audio guy *carte blanche* to cut the scene if he/she hears any audio issues.

I also make it a habit to run multiple recorders on each scene. I like to do this as a backup to the 'live' microphone running into the camera. We own a few Zoom H4s, which are workhorses and easy to use, they make great audio backups. Don't be shy; nothing wrong with having three or four recorders set at different places on the set.

On our film *Early Grave*, we were shooting in a large, high ceiling room and had portable digital Olympus recorders hidden in the salad bowls. Good audio is crucial; you cannot fix bad audio without having to re-record it. You know ADR is an expensive and time-consuming process so make sure you get the best audio recording you can on location. This will save you time, money, and frustration in the editing process.

DOLLIES AND JIBS

Today, many of the studio-backed filmmakers have a theory that it's always important to keep the camera moving. Steadicams are common on film sets today. They create compelling shots. While I do agree with this theory about keeping your camera moving, it's a battle for you as the director to keep the film on schedule as well.

Dolly and jib shots not only take much more time to set up, they increase at least threefold the time it takes to shoot each scene.

Setting up and leveling off tracks and jibs can take hours. Dolly shots, while important, will take much more production time.

TRUE STORY:

Our director of photography for *Willow Way,* Mike Boucher, a great DP and good friend, wanted to dolly across the entire set on the campfire scene to keep the camera moving. We had two people talking at a campfire. It could get very boring, so I reluctantly agreed to the dolly shot. After all, as the director I had to look at the big picture. It was getting dark, we were shooting between two large ponds, and it was a warm muggy night. Shooting in Maine in the summer is not for the weak. We had never seen so many mosquitoes in our lives. Couple that with the fact we could not run the generator because it was too loud. We had to fire up power inverters to our Jeeps and run a couple lights from the engines. It was by far the longest most uncomfortable scene I have ever shot in a film. The entire crew had to wear hoodies and bandanas so we didn't get bit. We brought dozens of cans of bug bomb and blasted the area. The set up took two hours and we were in the middle of the forest being eaten alive by some of Maine's finest mosquitoes. In the raw footage, you can see where we had to stop takes because all you could see were mosquitoes flying in front of the lens. The point here is to use dolly shots sparingly and only when you have the time to do them.

Pick three or four scenes in your movie where a moving dolly shot will enhance that shot. This is not Hollywood, you don't have the budget to make your camera move on every shot. In fact, that would be more distracting than not moving the camera. Pick the shots that would enhance the mood of that scene. A well-placed dolly shot will give you a professional look. Dolly shots in the low budget world work best as establishing shots or in scenes that are mostly dialogue. Moving the camera will help keep your audience from getting bored during a scene with conversation. These shots can be very powerful but very time-consuming so plan any dolly and jib shots well.

CAMERA STABILIZER

Another quick way to keep your shots moving and cut your setup time is to use a camera stabilizer. They are much more stable than hand-holding and much faster than dolly and jib shots.

My two favorite camera stabilizers are the halo rig, which is amazing and an inexpensive camera rig to use. Jon, the owner, is a great guy and another one of our film sponsors. Tell Jon you heard about him from this book. He can set you up with a nice rig for the camera you own. The site is www.halorig.com. We shot an entire feature film using two halo rigs. They are very light, and while they may look simple, they provide serious stabilization.

Another stabilizer to consider is the more expensive Blackbird, which is about six hundred dollars and well worth every penny. The Blackbird will take some practice to get used to. It is pretty easy to use right out-of-the-box. The Blackbird website is www.camotionllc.com . Rich, the president of Camotion Research, can answer any questions you have. The Blackbird is very stable and gives you great, smooth looking shots while you are moving. You can see examples on You Tube. The great thing about the Blackbird is that it costs far less than a steadicam rig and works just as well.

There are many stabilizers out there; be careful what you buy. A good stabilizer will take hours of practice to get the balance and movement right. In the long run you should be able to save time on the set using a stabilizer in place of a dolly or jib. In each case they will all make your film a bit more exciting; don't be afraid to try them and experiment. The worst thing that can happen is you don't use that footage.

SLIDERS

Sliders are new to the low budget filmmaker. Sliders have been in use in Hollywood for years. Because of the cost of a slider rig, indie filmmakers never really could afford one in their equipment case. Now, it's a different story. Just as the DSLR came around so did lightweight DSLR equipment. The DSLR slider is easy to use when you need to get a little movement in the shot. They are very small and lightweight and much easier to set up than a dolly system. Sliders come in various sizes three, four, five, and six feet. Using a slider, you can get the appearance of the beautiful dolly shot without lugging heavy tracks and platforms around. Some good sliders can be found and technology is getting better every day. The best thing about using a slider is that you can mount your slider to your tripod, which you will already have with you. DSLR sliders are perfect on the low budget and allow you to get working with a small crew and keep shots moving giving you production value. Sliders are a wonderful invention and easy equipment to carry around in the field.

CREW

We work with high school students, college students, AV students and established cinematographers. Your crew will be made up of many different people. Some indie filmmakers use very small four man crews, some like having one person for each job. That really depends on your budget and the talent pool you have around you. The best way to put together a crew is referrals; using people who worked for people in the business. Other filmmakers and actors will know people who love to shoot and take pride in what they do. They will also know the egomaniacs who want to direct your movie and consider themselves experts. Remember: Talk is cheap. Always get a referral from people before you work with someone you don't know.

TRUE STORY:

A couple of years back, after the sale of our second feature film, we thought it would be nice if we gave something back to the filmmaking community, so we reached out to all the local filmmakers and video production people with the hopes of creating an indie filmmaking workshop. The concept would be that I would teach a few seminars on getting distribution and dealing with distributors, perhaps one on editing. We would then bring in other regional filmmakers, sound people, makeup artists, DPs and lighting techs and have a weekend where we had experts in each area talking about their success and what they needed to do to master their specific skill. The admission would cover all the classes and we would split any money with the others teaching the classes. Months of preparation went into this expo, as we called it. Living outside Boston, we thought this would be a big hit with all the people who wanted to brush up on techniques or to learn about distribution. The one thing we failed to recognize:

Everyone is an expert in making movies.

Let me repeat that for you: Everyone is an expert in making movies. It doesn't matter that not one of the filmmakers in our area has any kind of professional experience and half never even finished a movie. They all know how to make movies and they are all experts.

That became evident when we started selling tickets to the event. We decided to pre-sell tickets three months ahead of time. What we found was that people actually questioned us. We heard bizarre comments like:

Why should I pay you to teach a class in filmmaking when I've already made a movie? I am a director. I already know the process.

Just to remind you, this entire expo idea was to help other filmmakers, audio engineers, photographers, actors, and editors get a better understanding of what was needed to make a commercial film for sale. We had just signed our second worldwide distribution deal. We were and still are leap years ahead of the others. With our network we had tons of inside information to share. We were not only shocked that people who call themselves filmmakers would not keep an open mind to learn new things, they were arrogant enough to challenge all of our teaching experts, myself included.

After selling only two dozen tickets out of our goal of three hundred, I pulled the plug on the expo concept. I decided it was every man and woman for themselves. We continue to sell movies and they just talk about it. Everyone is an expert in making movies, yet none of them have deals.

We didn't expect that kind of response. I shut down the expo site; I thanked all the teachers who were willing to share their experiences. From that point on we vowed we would not give out anymore inside information or help others who were not open minded or were ungrateful. The point here is you are going to find people who think they know everything. They know how to shoot and they know how to edit. Do what I do: call them out on it. Ask for a reel. Have them shoot or edit something for you. People in this business talk the talk, but rarely walk the walk. Call them out on everything they claim they can do. Nothing will give you more pleasure than seeing a big mouth eat its words.

NOTE: Putting together the right crew is like putting together an orchestra; all have to do their part. The most important factor on any crew is chemistry and how everyone will work together. It's crucial you evaluate this during your weekly meetings. Listen and you will soon see who just talks. Evaluate who is just talking to be heard or who has actual, beneficial information. Get rid of the talkers now. There will be plenty of those, so get rid of the people who think they know it all and get rid of those people immediately. A good source of dedicated crew people will be students in college-level film and video production classes; also, people who work in local TV and radio. Carefully screen potential crew members. Many times you will work long days for no pay. Be nice to them and take care of your crew. If you do have a budget, pay your crew first and always give them perks like hats, T-shirts and let them eat well.

NOTE: Be very careful when dealing with audio personnel. Just because some are radio DJs on the weekend does not mean they can record location audio. Spend some time with your sound people and get to know their strengths and weaknesses. Find out where their heads are. Are they doing this because they love the filmmaking process or are they doing this to pick up chicks?

When you have found the chemistry of your crew, you want to have the same crew for all your films. Our makeup supervisor, Amanda, has been with us from the beginning and I cannot imagine shooting a film without her. She knows the how, what and when of our productions. She is an important part of our filmmaking process.

NOTE: Ask others in the business who was good to work with, who's fun and has a good personality.

Look at college students; they make good crew members. Make sure there is chemistry with all your crew and your cast members. Prepare your crew for hard work and long hours; they may not know how long or how hard it is to make a movie, so make sure they understand this. Always try to find money and perks for your crew to keep them happy. This could be in the form of hats, T-shirts, pens, and other swag. Make sure you always feed your crew well and take care of them; they are the people who are going to help you get this project done.

THINKING AHEAD

Thinking ahead is a major part of the filmmaking process. In the beginning stages, even before you shoot one frame of video, you need to start thinking distribution. Yes, distribution. You want and need to have a clear pathway as to where you want your film to end up before you even shoot it. Many, if not most new filmmakers, will get overwhelmed once shooting begins. When you have all the footage shot, it will seem like you have a jumbled mess of takes and scenes. Don't panic, you will need to evaluate if you have a sellable commercial film. The value of thinking distribution before shooting helps keep you focused on the target.

What is the genre of my film?

Who will go to see my film?

What small distributors would carry my genre?

How can I make my film stand out over others like it?

Does my film have enough production value?

Can you see it on the screen?

Is it a commercial movie or more of an art film?

Visualize your project. Make plenty of notes and lists of distributors to call. IMDB Pro is a great resource for finding distributors and their addresses. Know what genre your film is classified; will it be able to cross over into other genres? Thinking ahead about potential distributors who may purchase your film is crucial at this stage.

TRUE STORY:

Some years back I met a filmmaker who wanted to make his own movie. I didn't think much of it; we shared ideas and brain stormed. I had already sold one film and was working on our second feature, *Back to the Beyond*. We would try to get together on a regular basis but time was tight for both of us. Trying to be a good friend I would tell him some of the pitfalls he was up against when the time came to sell his film, assuming he would even be able to finish it. A large chunk of time went by when we did not talk much and we were about ready for production on our second feature. They had editing issues with their film and could not find anyone who could truly edit a feature film. We went into production and finished our film while they were still working on theirs. In fact, I had almost finished editing *Back to the Beyond* when I got a call that they had finished their movie. I was happy they actually finished the film. I sat down with them. I told them what they should do next to get a screener prepared I could send to our distributor contacts. It was not long after that we secured our second film deal. I was still waiting for their screener. It was a few weeks later and along came their screener. I put it in the DVD player and immediately knew no one was going take this seriously as a commercial film. In the meantime I had alerted a few distribution contacts that I was sending over this film. (Never anticipate the completion of a movie). I should have waited until it was completed and up to specs. After viewing the screener I told them what the problems were, i.e., audio was bad, over dubs out of sync, music didn't fit and it would not pass the quality control test distributors put each film through. I told my contacts the film was being fixed and sent them a link to the trailer. I had no idea how long it would take for them to fix the problems. A few weeks went by, then a few months before I finally got the call they had made the corrections to their film and were sending me a new screener. I waited for the fixed version. While some of the edit changes were made to the film, I still could not see it passing the QC. I decided to send it as it was and let them deal with the distributor themselves. After all, they would have to pay to have the problems fixed if they wanted a deal. That was all irrelevant. When I called my contacts asking them if they wanted to see the screener I had promised them a couple months ago, they all said no, too late now. The filmmakers were not prepared. They didn't know what genre it would be classified, did not have music ready and their best guess was they would wait until the film was edited before they could even tell you if it was good. They just shot the movie and did not plan for anything else. Needless to say, it was never sold and barely made a couple film festivals.

NOTE: Most filmmakers are content to wait and see how the film turns out before they do any marketing on their movie. By not taking the aggressive approach, you are wasting valuable time. You are also being reactive instead of proactive. You should know what your film is about, the story, and the plot. If you can't pitch your own film, no one will be able to.

The biggest advice here is you will need to finish your film and do it right. You only get one shot at distributors. Not finishing your film gives you a credibility problem.

Distributors will not consider you and your film professional if you cannot keep your word.

Make lists of contact names and emails. One event we found very helpful was the American Film Market (AFM) held in Santa Monica, CA, each year. The American Film Market hosts distributors, sellers, and sales agents from around the world. It can be a costly trip, but you will be able to make serious contacts. You will get a good idea what kind of films distributors are looking for and what is actually selling. AFM has everybody under one roof.

CHAPTER 4

PRODUCTION

Okay, so here we are. We've spent the last six weeks or so organizing, planning, and getting prepared for the big shoot ahead. If you're like us, your rendezvous spot will be looking more like a Boy Scout camping trip than a film shoot. Tents, coolers, suitcases, and ten different vehicles loaded down with equipment. Air conditioners strapped to car roofs, chairs, inflatable beds, just about everything and anything you will ever need to make a comfortable home base for your shoot. During pre-production you hopefully made checklists and made sure different people are responsible for certain areas. This is the easiest way to organize and have others take some of the responsibility off your shoulders. It's amazing the things each individual needs on location, especially the cast and their wardrobes. While you are loading up the vehicles, you shouldn't be shocked how much stuff everyone is bringing. Just the cast alone will each have a couple of suitcases. When I talk about a load up, this is assuming you are going on location for a number of days. If you are making day trips then this does not become as big an issue. Coordinating personnel and vehicle load up is an exhausting job. It's chaotic and you still have to get to your home base and unload all these vehicles.

Everyone on our set—cast, crew or otherwise—is required to carry equipment and gear. This means tents, coolers, tripods and lights, whatever needs to be carried. No one is above this.

You get everyone settled in, equipment and gear unloaded; the trip is exhausting; what is first? The first order of business is having a huge production meeting once everyone is calm.

NOTE: This is the most important meeting you will have. At this meeting, you will set the tone for the entire shoot. You go over your locations, the scenes you will shoot, the rules of the house, and what everyone will do.

NOTE: Everyone is wide-eyed and excited; energy is flowing at this meeting. You will have everyone's undivided attention. Keep them pumped up. You are the general, now make this speech count. Explain what you will and will not tolerate. At this point everyone's ready to lay down their lives for you. Set the rules. You know what you have to do and you know how you want everyone to act. Explain the difficulties you will encounter on the shoot. Tell them you have an open door to talk to you about a problem. Make sure everyone respects the cast and crew.

On every film, I have the same rules. We use a guideline that works for us:

Crew call is at 7 a.m. (that means make sure they're in the makeup chair at 6:30 a.m.

No one is ever late to a meeting (not tolerated).

No one ever calls the other crew or cast members a name or insult.

Everyone carries gear. EVERYONE. (That means cast and crew).

One PA is always assigned to the director.

Everyone pitches in for cooking and cleaning (if you're on location).

Make sure this is done. Actors and crew are all on the same team. Prepare yourself for the first day or two of production; it will suck. People will trip all over themselves.

NOTE: Don't get frustrated on the first day of production; it will be slow. In fact, it will be very slow. It will seem like no one's ready. That is normal on the first day of production. Schedule your first shoot day as an easy day or half-day to get everyone up and running and on the same page.

Like a football team, your crew needs to jell and get up to speed. Watch all your crew members in action, see how each other works. You have to remember the DP needs to know what the PAs know, the actors need to see how you work with your crew, make-up needs to know the cast, the AC needs to know how the DP works. A production crew has many moving parts; relationships need to be forged from the very first day of the production. Everyone needs to get up to speed and that only happens with practice. I can't tell you how many times at the end of the first day's shoot I've said to myself, "I will never get this finished." I realized the crew just like a team before a game needs to stretch out. Let them get their production legs on day one. That's why it is easier to go with an easy shoot or half-day shoot. You will not see a huge improvement from day one to day two. By day three you will begin to start making your day and seeing that, yes, these people can work together.

NOTE: Making your day is a Hollywood term that means shooting a set number of pages for that day. Making your day in Hollywood terms means shooting around 6-8 pages per day. In the real world of low budget filmmaking, it means 8-12 pages a day. We have shot up to 12 pages per day. Indie filmmakers are always on a tight schedule; shooting eight pages a day is normal.

Day two will be a bit more work, but you will see by the end of the day who's going to work and who you may have to push. I hope you won't have to give a stern warning to anyone. Use their excitement and energy to work for you.

Day three and four should actually begin to flow like a machine. You now have had time to get into a rhythm, work together and have had a few beers together. Everyone is in harmony. In our case, we had a few days to get together relaxed and had some good food and a few drinks together. This is a good time to introduce everyone and just relax and get to know each other.

Do not prevent your cast and crew from blowing off some steam.

Do not be a hard ass on them once you wrap for the day.

Artists need to unwind and leave their minds every now and then. From this point on production should become second nature. You now have the daily routine and schedule in place. Post the schedule. The daily food schedule and location schedule needs to be posted where everyone can see, perhaps on the refrigerator or in the living room.

Soon you are going to see signs that things may start to falter. It may be grumblings from a PA, actor, or actress. Do not ignore them; these are the first signs of cracking in the foundation. You have worked so hard to get here, now make sure you can stay here.

NOTE: You are always going to have an issue with an actor, actress, or crew member, they are people too. (Hard to believe, right?) They are not normal people though. What usually happens at this point is that everyone has his or her confidence back. Perhaps even their cockiness; they can see a movie is actually being made. Find out what the issue is.

TRUE STORY:

On every shoot you will have one person who seems to rub people the wrong way. It may not be the intent of that person. It just may be that person is the square wheel. I have too many stories on this subject. Nevertheless, I will pick the one that could have really caused a major issue if not stopped in time. We had one actress who refused to contribute to the house duties, leaving dishes in the sink, not cooking or helping to keep the house clean, that type of stuff. I usually stay in different accommodations away from the cast and crew. I always set up one person to be a crew mom or dad. The last thing you need in a house full of actors is a diva. Come to find out this actress would not pull her weight, complained about being sick all the time, and really angered the rest of the cast and crew. They had set up a nice system for chores and meals. To me this had to be such a small problem it could be fixed quickly. To the cast and crew this was a huge issue.

Take these issues seriously.

This is where you need to take every issue as a major problem. Seems no matter how hard they talked to this person, she would become increasingly more stubborn. You go into your film knowing these are adults and they can settle their differences. Or at least you hope they can. It was about day four when I was asked for a closed-door meeting by two of the cast members. I was updated on this situation and how bad it had actually gotten. I had dropped the ball. I brushed it off as a little tiff they could settle. What actually happened is fights were breaking out between some of the girls and this diva. I had no idea they actually hated this girl. This issue now had to be the number one priority. At that night's meeting, I asked what the hell was going on, using a bit harsher language. To their credit, the cast spoke up and was honest about this person and what she was or was not doing. After some bickering and temper flares, I let the moment of silence linger while I walked around the room quietly. I turned to her and asked, "Why do you feel like you don't need to contribute." A simple question, right? She was a very nice girl; perhaps she was having some personal issues. Her answer could not have been more wrong for the situation. While I don't remember her exact words it came out as something like, "These guys are all full of shit and I don't take orders from them." I paused a moment and asked her if she was in charge. I was not ready for her second answer: "I'm here to act, not to be anybody's gopher. I will do my job and I don't need them or you telling me what I need to do." The room fell silent. A bit character was challenging me on my film. I tried to be calm; I mean I really had to fight to stay calm. I composed myself for a few seconds then I realized little miss diva needed to be brought back into the real world. I was white hot and at the top of my voice, I yelled, "Who the (bleep) do you think you are? This is my (bleeping) film and you work for me. Don't you ever challenge me on my set. You have five minutes to apologize to everyone in this room or you are off this set so fast your (bleeping) head will spin." Now you could hear a pin drop. I was never so mad at a cast member in all my years in production. I walked out to the porch, and cooled down. I talked with Laura, my executive producer, production manager and my right hand woman. Laura was one of the most organized people I had ever met and perfect for our production. Coming from an office management background, I knew she would be perfect. Laura could combine speed, quick thinking and management on a feature film we had to shoot in nine days. When I walked back in, I found our diva had left the room crying. I stood in the middle of the room and said to the rest of the cast and crew, "We are going to solve this issue now." I sent one of the PAs to get our diva. She came back humbled, crying and sorry for pissing me off. She promised she would become a member of the team.

From that point on, I had no further issues. She actually became quite a trouper. While the others still did not like her, we were all able to get along and finish the film.

Nine out of ten times it will be a cast member who needs an attitude adjustment, but not always.

Crew members just love to make movies; they don't care about being on camera. Complement them and make sure you get them a beer at the end of the shoot. Tell them how well they did and that the footage looks great. If you do that, they will take a bullet for you. I started out as a shooter/editor, so I always associated with the crew anyway. My crew members all know where I started and we share the same love of the filmmaking process.

YOU THE DIRECTOR

Two types of directors:

The technical type.

The character priority type.

While there is no right or wrong way to direct a movie, some directors like to stay involved in the technical process, working alongside the DP and the ACs on lighting and shot placement. Other directors give priority to the actors and let the crew deal with the technical aspects of the shoot. They like to work with the actors primarily on line delivery and movement. Coming from a technical background, I like to work on the technical side of things. I work closely with the DP and I like to set up my own lighting at times as well. If you decide to go that route you will need to have a strong AD and casting supervisor to work with the actors.

Being a director means many things. However, what it really means is you are the general contractor. You need to get your people in place and let them do their jobs. The most important thing you can do as a director is to let them have room to create. A few things you need to do as a good director:

Find the best people available.

Don't squeeze your cast; let them have room to change the words or say things differently from the script.

The script is just a guideline. It may not fit each character or the characters they create. Trust their instincts and let them go with the flow. Give them an open option to decide what is more important to that character.

Be ready to problem solve at some point.

Without question, many things will go wrong on a shoot. Perhaps you just have to fix something simple like running out of gas for the grill or losing a light and needing a bulb. Be ready, things happen on shoots. Some things happen that you could not even imagine.

TRUE STORY:

Many years ago while shooting in New Hampshire, we assembled a small rag tag crew to shoot an anthology. Since we were in New Hampshire with no money, we had to find people willing to work for nothing and still help us get the job done. We brought in a guy who worked in radio sales to do audio for us. We called him Stache. He was a nice guy. He had a sour marriage and needed to get away weekends, so working on a movie was perfect for him. When we first started out, we would shoot guerilla, no insurance, no permits, nothing.

We had a shoot scheduled for the shoreline. We all gathered at a little café, completed our shoot and had made plans to rendezvous at our friend Mary's house to spend the night. Everyone made it back to the house except Stache (this was before cell phones). We had no idea what happened to him. He also had one of our PAs, the girl the guys went gaga over. She went with Stache to ride back to Mary's house. A couple of hours passed before he finally returned. He had a bandage on his chest and we asked what the hell happened? Turns out Stache had broken down just after leaving the shoot, his car had overheated. He pulled over on the side of the road and decided to look at the engine. While Stache was a nice guy, he certainly was not the brightest bulb in the marquee. Turns out he opened the radiator cap while the engine was hot and got scalded by antifreeze all over his chest. He spent the next two hours at the emergency room. When I say anything can happen on a production it really can.

That being said, people are not going to be the only problem-solving issue. Equipment breaks all the time. Make sure you have a MacGyver type on your set who can work wonders with duct tape. When you are on location, make note:

Know where the local ER room or clinic is.

Know where local mechanic is.

The local supermarket.

The local police and fire stations.

Make a map or have a local help you draw a map where all these things are. Sure, you may never need them. However, you might. I have a saying I use all the time:

"It is better to have it and not need it than need it and not have it."

As the director, you personally will not have time to socialize as much as you think. You need to have nightly meetings after each shoot day with your DP and AD to go over the next day locations. When you come back from the set that day grab some food, you will still have work to do. Your day as the director is not over. While your cast and crew are relaxing and going over their lines you will have meetings and you still have to view the dailies from that day's shoot. You will also need to address any cast issues you may have.

You will be the first guy to the set and the last guy to leave.

You must set the example, make sure it's a high bar to follow.

One of the directors' friends in this age of filmmaking is accessing digital footage quickly. We have instant access to our footage. That's the good news. The bad news is that with one push of the wrong button we can also erase an SD card forever. Always prepare extra hard drives. Bring extra hard drives and have a PA or technical DI make backups of backups.

NOTE: One thing I do is have a technical PA transfer the dailies to two, three or four different hard drives, one for me, one for the DP, one for each assistant director. When we leave the location we have identical drives at different locations. Back up, back up, and back up. If one drive goes bad, you always have the others. You can also make backups of your hard drive once you get home.

This is digital so no resolution loss occurs when making copies.

Better to have it and not need it than need it and not have it. This goes for audio as well. If you are running external audio recorders, make sure you back up each recorder to a drive and have separate audio folders as well.

THE DAILY GRIND

Sleep will be a luxury on your film. You will wake up early and go to bed late. You and your cast and crew will walk around like zombies all in the name of making a movie. The best advice here is coffee. Lots of it and all the time. If you don't drink coffee, now is the time to start.

From a practical standpoint, if you start shooting early the more shots you can get in during the day. A good early crew call is 7 a.m. That should be the latest you start shooting. Make sure your cast is told they need make up 30 minutes before crew call. Always have fruits, coffee, and water available throughout the day, not just in the morning for the cast and crew. As an athlete in my early years, I have a background in nutrition. Knowing what foods are good and bad helped us figure out what would be best for the cast and crew to eat.

NOTE: Always avoid pastas and pizzas for lunch. Anything that has carbohydrates will turn to sugar very quickly. You will find your cast and crew nodding off by 2 o'clock. Plan accordingly. Low carbohydrates at lunch. Moreover, as I stated before, always have fruits and drinks available throughout the day.

THE WALK THROUGH OR BLOCKING

The walk through of your film will be the official start of principal photography. In your first walk through you will create movement for your actors, the DP will be able set up the shots and lighting, and the sound crew will know where to place the boom to stay out of the shot. This is also called blocking the shot. This is your practice run-through. Give your actors marks to hit, have a crew member take still photos. This is when everyone can visualize the scene. The DP and AC will decide where to place lights and dolly tracks to go from point to point. Blocking is also the time when you as the director and the DP (if not the same) look at camera placement, shoot angles and lens lengths. You will also become aware of your surroundings to avoid shooting into doors and windows. The cast will practice their movements and how they move across the room.

Hire a good DP and AC (director of photography and assistant cinematographer). Production lighting technology is another element overlooked or bypassed entirely. Good lighting should look natural, like there is no extra lighting source at all. The art of lighting takes years to perfect.

CROSSING THE LINE AS THE DIRECTOR

At some point during the shoot, you will be tested as a director. You will need to make snap decisions to avoid looking like a fool. These snap decisions will catapult you into leadership or drop you into the bullshitter category.

You as the director has to know EVERYTHING ALL THE TIME.

How do you do that? Well, I will tell you. You won't know everything all the time, but you make everyone think you do. The thing to remember is you are the director, you are in charge. This is not a democracy; you don't need to vote on decisions. You are expected to know everything that goes on. You need to present yourself as the general. A few things you never do:

You never ask for help.

Never ask for advice in front of others.

You always have the answer or you will get it.

If you are wrong, admit your mistake and move on quickly. You always know what you're doing; you have a handle on everything.

I definitely learned this the hard way and screwed up a few times. I thought that with such a knowledgeable cast and crew I would invite democracy. I thought feedback might be helpful and some great ideas may come from our people.

Wrong. Once you open that door, everybody will walk in and everybody has a better idea.

Everybody knows how to direct your movie. Do not open that door. When I say, do not cross the line, it is much easier said than done. It may be something that slipped your mind, we all slip and make mistakes. It's what you do afterward that counts.

TRUE STORY:

I think it was close to midnight on an exhausting fourteen-hour day. Everyone was tired; the coffee pots were going full boil. Two shots left to make our day. In a total mind fart, I completely crossed the line. Right after completing the shot in my haste and not thinking, I said let's reset the lights for the table shot. As soon as I said that, I knew I had crossed the line and made a crucial error in judgment. I had to jump back quickly or look like an idiot. I totally forgot about the reverse angle and over the shoulder shots (OTS) for that last take. It was late, we were all dragging. I walked away and expected to see the AC and PAs breaking down the lights, but no one was moving. Suddenly the DP shouts to them from across the room, "Wait, don't touch the lights, we need the reverses." Everybody stopped, the cast and crew were waiting see my response; all eyes were on the director. Resetting the lights meant another forty-five minutes of set up time. I screwed up and now it looked like I didn't know what I was doing. As everyone waited for my directive, I asked my great PA, Anja, to get me a coffee. As I had done so many times before to others, I was being called out on my decisions. I had to think quickly. I suddenly remembered watching the dailies the night before and saying to myself, *I am so glad we did the cool overhead shots, they will cut in nicely.* They were shots I could use in place of doing reverses. Putting in that extra work the night before helped me find the answer to the problem. Everyone was still looking at me as Anja brought my coffee. They all wanted to see if the great DiBacco screwed up and what to do next. I now knew exactly what I was doing; I was prepared and thought ahead from the night before. I broke out in a laugh. "Remember last night?" I asked. "When I asked you guys to climb the loft and get the overhead shots?" A collective nod from the crew. "That's what I'm using instead of the reverses." "Great idea," the DP said. Everyone approved, we all love those shots. Even though they had more work to do, they relaxed and I had saved myself from looking like a fool. One of the crew even threw a zinger my way when he yelled to me, "Shit, Kev, you know what you are doing, huh?"

My point is, be ready to jump back once you have crossed that line. Never leave doubt in the minds of your cast and crew that you are the big dog in charge. Don't let on you've crossed the line, just get back quickly. You will find once you have directed long enough, you will be able to handle this problem much better. You will also be less likely to put yourself in that situation by being prepared.

Be strong and know you are in charge. You have to make snap decisions without losing any credibility or respect. Allow no politics on a shoot, don't let your set become a democracy. This is a dictatorship and you are the dictator. Things can get out of hand quite quickly, things you should have seen coming.

One ridiculous concept I have seen is director collaboration: Filmmakers who try to be best friends and go with two and three directors on one film. Seriously? Do not let that happen. It is like having three CEOs run a corporation.

One voice, one director.

If you need help, have an assistant director (AD). I don't even believe in a second or third co-director. The multiple director idea has to be the dumbest thing I have ever heard. One voice, one director.

Production is not an open discussion forum. Being in charge also means acting professionally. Never belittle your cast or crew for mistakes. Nothing is worse for morale, and you don't want to become the asshole director who dictates too much and makes people feel like shit.

In time, with tons of practice, you will come up with a system that works for you. A shoot is a shoot; for the most part, they are all the same. It's the way you organize a shoot that makes it more efficient. I am not afraid to say we have made all kinds of mistakes making our movies. The biggest difference between Hollywood and us is they are able to throw money at the problem, but we have to find a fix without money. My hope is you will see what we have encountered and save yourself time and money on the production of your film.

THE 'POP UP' GREEN ROOM

The biggest advice I can give you about keeping noise away from the set when shooting is don't have the actors too close to the set. Laughing and talking will certainly screw up your takes and test your patience as a director. Keep the cast and extras not needed far away from the actual set where you are shooting. Because we are working in the low budget world we cannot offer the cast a trailer to work out of, so we do the next best thing, a pop up tent or gazebo.

We like to set up a recreation area both inside and outside where cast can go to relax when not in that scene. We usually purchase a gazebo tent and have it stocked with coolers of water and coffee urns. The key here is to make it far enough away from the shoot where you cannot hear anyone talking.

TRUE STORY:

We have encountered this noise problem on every shoot we have ever had. The smaller the building, the worse the problem. When shooting *Back to the Beyond* we were all inside a small cottage on the shoreline. There was really only one place for the extra cast to go—a big tent we had set up in the far corner of the yard. I was constantly yelling to the cast to be quiet and after several times I decided to put a PA out there to make sure they stayed quiet. It was always the same one or two people having a jolly old time. Nothing is more frustrating than having to stop a scene because you hear people outside laughing and joking. The best thing you can do, as a rule, is to have the non-essential cast stay away from the set until needed. Keep them at the hotel or make sure they are as far away from the set as you can get them. There will be times when you are all stuck in a cramped area. This may be the time when you have to shuttle them to and from the set or to a café. The best way to avoid this problem is no extra people on the set at all if they are not in that scene.

Some other rules we put in place to keep noise off our set:

Don't have different PAs running on and off the set.

Dedicate one PA as a runner between you and your cast.

Don't let anyone have a cell phone on the set.

Don't let the cast make special requests.

When things begin to unravel a bit have everyone take five.

During scheduled breaks, it is okay to let the cast and crew use their phones. Never during the shoot. All cell phones are off. Often people leave their cell phone on and in their pockets. Do not let this happen. This includes your cell phone. Be sure you have the craft services area for your cast and crew, as we touched on earlier. The one thing you never do during a shoot is let the cast make special requests for specialty food.

This is not Burger King; they don't get it their way.

There will be times when the chaos level starts to rise. Don't just walk off the set or show any kind of disgust. Simply tell the cast and crew to take five so all can regroup. If you have something that really bothers you, just take five and then calmly deal with it. You as the director always have to stay calm.

In your pop up tent or craft services area you want the cast to feel comfortable, so have enough chairs and tables as well as refreshments. Keep coffee and juices going all day. Keep on schedule as close as possible. Lunch is very important, but stay on schedule.

Always offer encouragement during all breaks to both cast and crew. A few kind words from their fearless director will keep the excitement and momentum going.

Have a PA bring water and/or coffee to the cast and crew who are stuck on the set and unable to get to the craft services tent. The last thing you want to do is stop momentum once the scene starts flowing. Bringing refreshments to them will help keep the flow and keep your actors in character.

LATEX EFFECTS AND PROPS

Unless you are making coming of age or love stories for your entire career, you will undoubtedly need blood effects: stab wounds, cuts, scrapes, gunshots, etc. Some of these effects can be done in post-production with good effects software, some cannot. You will need to have real props like rubber knives and realistic guns. Air soft makes some realistic prop guns you can purchase online. You can also purchase rubber knives that need to be painted to look real. Fortunately, we had Eric Anderson, an effects expert who lived near us. We hired Eric to create our blood effects, wounds, and props. On a small budget it is almost impossible to make some of these effects look real. You need someone who knows this craft.

NOTE: If you cannot make any type of effect on screen look realistic, don't do them at all.

It is much better to take a page from Hitchcock and insinuate or hint something happened than to have an unrealistic, bad effect. When you get to the stage where you will be doing gunshots, bullet wounds, cuts, and scrapes you are much better off hiring someone who can work with latex materials and knows the business. We made the mistake of thinking we could do these in house on our own and we failed to make it look realistic. Another lesson we learned the hard way.

You can always find people in your area who are into that end of filmmaking. Work out a deal with them and let them do their thing.

MAKE UP

Every television show and feature film requires make up. From your local news show to NBC sitcoms, make up is needed. Shooting HD video, make up is now more important than ever. We have had the same make up artist with us from the very beginning. Amanda is a real trouper and our go to girl for everything on our shoots. She has developed her skills over time and is being hired to do make up on many of the local productions and feature films in our area. We consider her part of the DiBacco Films family. Once you have found your make up artist, keep that person. You cannot just bring in a girl from the local JC Penney make up counter. If you can afford her, I'm sure she would be willing to work on your crew as well.

Since the introduction of high definition (HD) video cameras, cosmetics companies have scrambled to create a better make up that would look natural in the high definition format. HD was more than two times the resolution of standard definition video and on a big screen bad make up would be seen very quickly. The new 4K cameras and now the 8K cameras show incredible detail. Now everyone will notice wrinkles or scars, making any imperfections appear worse.

Make up is a skill set, and a very important part of film and television production. Interview various people to find out who knows people who have worked in the business. Make up is something you as the director have to take seriously. Find your own Amanda and never let her go.

SMART SCHEDULING

Smart scheduling really is a nice way of saying have back up plans among back up plans. Planning the small details ahead of time will save you money when you start scheduling. One of the most cost effective things you can do is to have the least number of cast members on the set at a given time. The three big reasons here are:

You have fewer people to feed.

You have fewer hotel rooms to pay for.

Fewer people means less confusion and less noise.

Breakdown your script with your AD by characters. What day will you need all the characters?

What locations will need all the characters?

The way we like to do this is have all the cast members on set the first four or five days. We then start shooting the scenes with fewer and fewer characters, until we have the minimum numbers of characters by the end of the shoot. By scheduling this way, you will save money.

I personally like to shoot the hardest scenes in the first four days, with the largest cast. You will never shoot a movie in sequence. It all depends on how you schedule. Scheduling falls onto the back of your AD and second AD. Let them work on a production schedule. They will be able to get the information from all the cast members, combine it with the location information and coordinate a schedule. You will have a definite time on some locations. For example, the diner will only let you shoot on Monday evenings from 9-11. You have to work backward and make sure the cast in that scene is available at that time. The AD and second AD will have the responsibility of scheduling. You have to be ready to help them should they reach a bottleneck. You as the director may even have to make phone calls to move locations around or have your super producer (ours was Laura) get it all worked out.

There some great programs out there and some you can use online to create a master calendar. They will be able to help you create a full schedule.

NOTE: Make sure they schedule in your fun time; for me it's our nightly ice cream pig-out with the PAs.

We have someone make a Ben & Jerry's run each night. Nothing more fun after a long days shoot than showing up, throwing on the sweat pants, then sitting down with the PAs and eating ice cream from the container.

REHEARSALS

Rehearsals are always difficult. People live in different towns or states. To schedule regular rehearsals with people who live in different areas, you will have to coordinate their travel. However, if you are lucky enough to have your cast close enough, order pizza and beer and go through a table read of the script. This becomes a problem when you have people living in different states. The best solution is to have rehearsals on location. Fact is the first thing we do before shooting is set up the rehearsal times and a walk through. We schedule rehearsals every day while on location. We find a convenient time, perhaps after dinner or before you go out to the set. You will be too busy to set up a rehearsal schedule so this should be completed by your second AD. Let him or her run rehearsals from this point on. The point of on location rehearsals is to prepare the cast for the next day of shooting. If any script changes are needed, now is the time to get them in the script. Make rehearsals fun, maybe with dessert, food, or a bottle of wine. This is when you want to iron out the mistakes before you get to the set. This is a great time to have everyone feel part of the team, so have fun with it.

DIRECTING YOUR ACTORS AND ACTRESSES

Your job as director also means being a psychologist, a mediator, a babysitter, a boxing trainer, and a drill sergeant all in one. Rehearsals are an excellent way to see where people are on the personality scale. The time you spend with your cast is very important. You have to keep them motivated, happy, and productive. One fact: actors and actresses are not logical thinkers. Be prepared to have one or two square wheels among your cast. You will hear comments like, "That's not how I used to do it," and, "That's not how it's done in the business" or "I never heard of it being done that way." Cut the head off that kind of talk immediately. Your reply to any type of comment that challenges you, as a director, should be simple and direct. "That's how it's done on my set."

You are the director, you are in charge.

Remember to define yourself. What kind of director am I? Am I going to be a technical director or a character priority director? I have learned and witnessed far too many directors having this God-like ego where they feel they have to control every aspect of the character. To me that is total bullshit.

Give your characters the space to create. Let them create in their own minds. Let them become the characters; let them perform the characters their own way. In other words, let them do their jobs. Don't control every word they say, let them improvise to fit their needs and their language. The script is only a guideline; words can be changed and at times should be changed in the script. Once I feel characters know who each character is and how to become that person, I let them become that person.

I rarely talked to cast members on the set. They have the characters they created in their heads; you have seen their creation. Unless, it is totally off base with what you think that character should be, let them have the freedom to run with it.

If you feel all your actors have created the proper characters for their parts let them create their art.

I never stop the flow of character interaction. Many directors are so insecure and have to show off that they constantly stop the scene with mundane directions. The entire point of directing is to get your cast to tell the story. If you have a director who feels like flexing his muscles on every take, you will find a production in chaos.

NOTE: Never stop momentum. Step back and watch. Everyone knows you are the director. You don't need to push the cast by making radical speeches during the middle of the shoot. Just sit back and watch them work. Always evaluate if they are telling the story correctly.

A good director knows when to be seen and when to shut up.

I believe you never smother your actors, they know their craft, and they have a skill. You brought them in to use their skill. Get them on the proper track, and they will take it from there.

DAILY FOOTAGE DAILIES

It is crucial you have a good tech guy or girl on today's HD shoots. Digital files are very fragile; once video files are erased, they are gone for good. Have a system in place for the archiving of daily footage. Fortunately, by shooting HD you have the ability to know instantly what your footage looks like. In the old days of film, you had to wait a day or two to get your dailies back. It was a painful wait.

Today we have access at any time to play back the raw footage. It's ready at any time to view. As I said before, watching the shoot footage from that day will also help you put this film together in your head, as well as see what you may have missed on that particular day. Dailies are always fun to view with everyone. We like to pull out some of the outtakes and show everyone at one time as a way to relax and have fun.

Make notes and keep a log. You will want to compare the rest of the footage to your dailies.

Archive your footage. The very first thing you should do is archive your footage to external storage drives immediately. The moment you get off the set, the first order of priority should be to get all your footage backed up. Make up all the backups multiple times.

Never, I mean never, erase the original SD cards until you have backed up all your footage on external hard drives and confirmed it is there.

Confirm the backup is viewable and exactly the same as the original files. Dailies have been used since the beginning of making movies. It's a valuable tool to evaluating and judging the progression of a motion picture. Use them to help you with your film and to guide you with the rest of the project.

FLEXIBILITY

In any occupation, business or personal, when dealing with organization, you have to be flexible. Life and business work best by scheduling and planning. More often than not getting off track happens to the best of schedules .Be sure to develop adaption skill to handle recurring unexpected situations. Always schedule enough pad time at the end of your day to make adjustments, like having a business meeting run too long and screw up the rest of your day. It happens on the shoot all the time. You must adjust quickly. Without fail, we have run into situations where we need to shoot outside only to have it raining on that day. This scenario presents a few problems. Swapping shoot days is fine but do you have the proper cast on the set to do so?

Leave yourself some flexibility in your schedule—you will run into this, no question about it. It may mean you may have to get everyone up an hour earlier the next day or just swap days altogether. There's no knowing what will happen, make sure you're flexible with the schedule and able to adapt at any time:

Be prepared to change locations if you have to.

Have a backup plan in a backup schedule.

Leave some extra time at the beginning and the end of your day.

Unlike Hollywood, you cannot just throw money at the problem; you have to be ready to think out-of-the-box. I like to call these unexpected problems the curve ball effect. Just as you are used to getting fastballs to hit, what happens when out of nowhere somebody throws a curve ball and you are not ready? I will tell you after being in this business for so long I have witnessed just about every production curve ball. People sent to the hospital, thrown out of their house, crew members arrested, family tragedies, business shut down during the shoot, owners arrested, managers arrested, backers pulled out at the last minute, crew member quitting. You name it and it can happen. Be ready for the curve ball.

TRUE STORY:

Just before writing this book I worked for nine months with my management company to secure funding for my next feature film. Weeks of fine-tuning our business plan, getting business letters written, financial documents filed. It was days and weeks of writing, getting all this information to my management company to present to overseas investors. After working so hard, I found I had not heard from my management company and I finally wanted answers. I decided to do some background checks on these people. I contacted other directors who were at one time represented by these guys. I heard many disturbing stories and no one I had talked to ever got any funding from them. After a little more digging on the players involved with this company I found out that one of their so-called officers had just been indicted for running a Ponzi scheme. After digging up the court records, it turns out all of them had served prison time for the same scheme and were attempting to do the same thing again. I do not need to tell you how frustrating and discouraging something like this is. What I have come to realize and you should adopt this as well:

Don't believe anyone who tells you he has money.

This entire business is built on bullshitters and liars.

More often than not people will talk the talk and never come close to walking the walk. If they have money let them show you or your attorney a good faith gesture. Let them put seed money in your account or let them get the funds into escrow. Keep saying to yourself: Show me the money…show me the money.

Money first. Never believe anyone offering you money. It just does not happen like that. I wasted months of time getting our package together; while it didn't cost much money, we wasted valuable time trying to find money from people who just didn't have the money to begin with.

That is the financing curve ball, and when it comes to funding, it will happen. It may be a small amount of funding or it may be big, but it will happen. You have to prepare for this curve ball, the bullshitters and the liars. I sum them all up as the Asstalkers because all they do is talk out their asses. You have no way of knowing who you are dealing with. You can do your research. You can find out who's actually a producer and who has access to money. Even with that, it does not mean they are not Asstalkers.

NOTE: Never, never, never put any of your own money up front to anyone promising you funding.

If they like your project, they will put money into your project. You never put money upfront no matter what they tell you they can do for you.

CHAPTER 5

POST-PRODUCTION

Without question, post-production or editing is the most important step in every film. I truly believe that:

The editor is the most important crew member on any film. It's not the director, it's the editor.

The editor makes the movie. The editor tells the story. The director just gets all the credit. Be thinking about the edit on day one of the film, especially if you are both the editor as well as the director.

Many Hollywood directors use the same editor to cut their movies for years and years and it becomes a professional and personal relationship. They know they can trust that person to translate their vision.

In my case, I started out as a shooter/editor. Everything I shot I had to edit. I took that thirty years-plus experience and skill into editing my own movies.

NOTE: Not everyone can edit a movie; long form editing is an acquired skill.

Short films and commercials will teach you how to keep the audience for a short time. A good editor has to know how to keep the flow of the film as well as the audiences' attention for ninety minutes or more.

A smart, experienced filmmaker will know where the movie is made. The movie is made in editing. As much as the director would like to think it's his work that created the film, I don't see it that way. I can say this because I have been both the director and the editor. The editor has to put all the pieces of the puzzle together.

Today in the digital world, you have tons of options to cut your film via computer. Desktops and laptops make great edit systems, and now even iPads can edit HD video. If you feel you are a good enough editor to take on this challenge, then make sure you have an edit system that works smoothly and without issues. We always edit on Macs, always have, and always will. Professional editors always use Mac-based systems such as Avid or Final Cut Pro.

Fear not my PC friends, a number of great editing programs exist for the PC as well. I have edited with and like Adobe Premiere and Sony Vegas. Adobe Premiere at one time offered the only edit software available. Premiere is a very professional editing program. To this day, I still keep Adobe Premiere on my Mac as well.

For the sake of your sanity don't get caught up in the platform or having to drop a ton of money into an edit system. Learn the craft of editing. Thousands of online tutorials can help you with the basic skills of editing. Just like anything else, the more you edit the better you become.

To start you just want to get comfortable putting scenes together. It's not creative editing; you just want to learn how to build a flow. You just want to tell the story. If this is your first film, reviewing thirty or forty hours of footage can get overwhelming. Many independent films die at this stage. Shooting the movie is the semi-glamorous part of production. Editing is the hard work.

The process for NLE or non-linear editing on a computer means all the footage you shot has to get digitized or transferred into a digital editing format. As you digitize your footage into your edit system, you need to stay calm and organized. Be patient, this is a long distance race; it's not a sprint.

Digitizing or transferring your footage into your system will take days if not weeks. You may only have to transfer the footage and transcode the files into a proper editing format. On the other hand, if you are shooting with a taped based format like HDV, you will have to actually digitize the takes you want to use. You do this by using an external video deck or camcorder. It's a mechanical process that has you starting and stopping at in-and-out points throughout your raw footage tape. Digitizing tape into your edit system is a long and drawn out process. As hard as it is, many professionals still do it. Newer cameras allow filmmakers to just drag files onto their hard drives from the SD card, re-encode them, and start editing quickly.

My favorite format and the format distributors like to get the master files in is ProRes 422. It's a professional codec developed by Apple. It has impressive image quality at reduced storage rates. It is virtually lossless and has very little compression. It looks great and is very easy on your processor. For the PC editing, this will be more of a challenge. There are ProRes 422 converters available; however other formats work equally as well like DVC Pro HD.

NOTE: The H264 myth. H264 is an acquisition format you shoot with. It's very processor intense and will slow down your system. You will need to transcode your original H264 footage into a clean editing format like ProRes 422 or DVC Pro HD format.

NOTE: The reality is you are not going to edit this film in a couple of weeks. Shoot for ninety days to edit the film, that's a good time frame and realistic. Start with simple assemble edits. An assemble edit is nothing more than laying down shots in order, just putting the scenes together. That is the easiest way to start editing. Watch all your raw footage, and take notes as to which are the best shots and which shots are not worth using.

NOTE: I hope you have taken notes when you watched your dailies. Bring that notebook and the script into your edit and have it with you all the time. Start with scene one of the movie, and drop in all your master shots in order. I even keep the slate in the timeline so you can see what you are actually editing. Scene one, shot one; scene 2, shot two, etc.

HARD DRIVE STORAGE

Editing HD footage will require you to have much more storage than was needed in the old SD (standard definition) days. Some great edit drives are on the market today. I would not worry about having to buy three thousand dollar RAID systems. You want to do your homework. Find drives that will work seamlessly with your edit system.

A RAID stands for (redundant array of independent disks), which really just means a bundle of hard drives acting like one super hard drive. Different kinds of RAID configurations do different things—one kind gives you crazy fast performance, another makes your storage safer than a single hard drive acting alone via redundancy.

NOTE: The thing you want to do is have a separate drive to edit on. This means attaching an external drive to your system via FireWire 800 or eSata. The new Macs are using the Thunderbolt/USB drives. Thunderbolt drives are very fast, but also very costly.

If you are a geek and don't mind taking apart your system to put in additional drives then by all means go for it. I find it easier and physically cooler for my Mac to edit off external drives. Personally I like the OWC drives sold by Other World Computing (www.macsales.com.).

They have been very reliable for me. The one thing I always do is set up a new drive for each new project. I store the last hard drive on the shelf. The last thing you want in the middle of your edit is a hard drive failure. I totally put my trust in the OWC Elite Pro Dual Drive RAID. They are fast, quiet and like I said, very reliable. I purchase one for every project. OWC also has a good reputation of customer support. While we have had drives fail us in the past, OWC was quick to replace them before we lost any data.

Another very popular drive with editors is the very fast and reliable G-Technology G Drives. They also come with a three-year warranty, which is very good. Both the OWC Elite and the G-Drive will work on either the MAC or PC platforms. I highly advise you to purchase one of these drives to edit on. You will note many other drives you can use to edit with. Be very fussy when choosing an edit drive. I have given you two worthy brands.

If you are trying to save money you can always find cheaper drives. My advice is to stay away from any kind of remanufactured or refurbished drive as your edit drive. These drives would be better suited as a back-up drive of your edit drive. A refurbished or remanufactured drive is not reliable enough to become your master edit drive.

CUTTING YOUR FIRST FILM TEASER

TEASER

One of the first things you want to edit is a very sharp teaser, something short, one minute or less. This will be a mini trailer for you to post online. You want to get people excited about your film; cutting a teaser will do just that. In fact, you can cut several teasers and replace them every month or so.

In Hollywood, you will see teasers that are most times cut before the movie is finished shooting. They put together the teaser from the first couple of days of shoot footage. Another thing they do is use stock footage. A teaser is a quick rough cut, nothing fancy. Many times a teaser won't even have effects. We have all seen Hollywood teasers of a film that has footage you never saw in the actual film. It happens all the time. A quick teaser is edited together before all the footage has been shot. You want to tell the audience the film is in the works. The teaser may simply be one scene from the film with graphics and music. This will all depend on how you want to market your film.

ASSEMBLE EDIT

What is an assemble edit? An assemble edit is nothing more than laying the scenes into the timeline in order. Nothing fancy, just straight cuts. All you want to do is lay out each scene from beginning to end. As said above, the most productive way to do this is to use all your master shots from each scene, editing them together back to back. Use all the best master shots for this assemble edit.

NOTE: Don't bother with the close-ups or the reverse angles for now. Don't bother with audio for now.

The assemble edit of master shots will take as long as two or three weeks, maybe a month. Don't rush it; this is the skeleton of the film. You will add the muscles and skin over the skeleton later on with each pass you make. In this scenario, you will be able to drop the close-ups and the reverse angles on top of the master shot to see how they fit. At the beginning stage, you will end up with the timeline of master shots in an order that will make up the entire film. This will put the whole film in perspective and give you an idea of the story and how it will cut together.

Don't bother tightening the edits. Don't bother with trimming the shots for now.

Once you have all the master shots assembled, you now have your first rough edit. This assembly edit is your first pass or first round of editing. You now can see the master shots you have to work with. If your shoot went well, your master shots will tell the story. You will enhance the story with your reverse shots, medium shots and close-ups.

The second pass of the film will be a second rough cut. Essentially in this next pass you will drop in the close-ups or medium shots throughout the time line. Your film will really now start to take shape.

Once you have the second rough cut done, you will get to the creative edits. From this point on you will try to place the perfect shots to compliment the master shots. You are now building the movie. This is where you try out the other shots so see how they fit together, like a puzzle.

Therefore, you make another pass with the medium shots, then another pass with the close-ups and see how they all fit together. By now, you have been editing a good five or six weeks. You are really creating a movie. With three or four passes, you have all the scenes in the proper sequence. You are still rough cutting. Odds are you will change shots all along the timeline in the next few weeks.

Now you can see how the film flows and the story is being told.

Is the story told correctly? Does it make sense?

You will constantly adjust shots, moving them around. By now the scenes should stand on their own.

NOTE: The biggest dilemma as an artist and a filmmaker is to know when you spend enough time editing your film. You could essentially edit your film for years. You can always find things to change, things you don't like. If you are compulsive, that may be a major problem for you. At some point, you have to let it go and trust you did the best you can with it.

TRUE STORY:

On my first film, I wanted to make it the best feature that I possibly could. Something to make people say, "Wow, they did a great job for what they spent." I constantly make rough cuts available for our DP Mike to review.

NOTE: Editing is like painting or writing, you will always have days where you just can't get into it, days where you are slow and don't have the creative energy.

As I edited our feature, I would find myself going back to scenes in the movie that the day before I liked and the next day I had to change. I'm not really sure what had happened. I developed some kind of compulsion to make each scene perfect. That was until the next day when I had to change it. This went on for weeks. Great scene three one day, the next day I had to re-edit scene three. Scene eight was perfect one day, the next day I had to re-edit scene eight. I could not figure out what was going on. I was obsessing over every little detail of the film. The worst part of it was we were on a schedule to finish the film before November 1, to take the film to AFM in California. Each day it became increasingly more frustrating. I would see the film different every time I watched it. I had to find out what this was. My first thought was okay, I just dumped a bunch of stocks to get the cash to make this movie so it has to be perfect. Money was a large part of it. This compulsiveness was new to me. I finally reached out to an editor I knew and told him the situation. This person had a couple features under his belt and he knew the process quite well. The advice I got was priceless and something I will turn around and give to you. He told me as an editor you can only work with what you have. Unless they are going to re-shoot scenes all you have is what is in front of you. Cut the shots together using the best shots. Make sure the scene makes sense then let it go. I told him I was trying to do that but kept going back into the timeline to do surgery. He calmly said to me, "Do the best with what you have to work with. You are not a magician, nor do you have the millions of dollars to make changes like Hollywood does." I already knew this; I knew I could not edit this thing forever. After all, I have been an editor for a long time. When my friend said it though, it made sense.

Edit what you have to work with, and then let it go. It all sank in. I could not make something out of nothing. I could only put the best shots in place and make them tell the story. It was evident that if I had not bounced this off another editor I would still be editing this film.

NOTE: The point here is that at some point you as an artist have to step back and say to yourself, "I did the best I could with what I had to work with." It may not be easy but you have to know when to walk away from a project. There has to be a point where the film is considered finished.

So making edit passes of your film is normal. No set rules exist on this. You keep making passes or edit rounds. You eventually will see the film develop before your eyes. Once you have all the video scenes in sequence then you will look at any CGI that may need to be done.

NOTE: Don't be afraid to get opinions. Show people the rough cuts and get the reaction of your wife, mom, husband, friends, and co-workers. Get opinions from people who watch movies. Feedback will give you knowledge.

NOTE: One way I look at my rough edits is I shut off all dialogue and just watch the visuals. No sound, no music, a silent movie. If you can understand the film while it's silent, then you know you will have a tight story once the dialogue, music and effects are mixed in.

Ask others who view the rough edit questions:

Does the movie tell the story?

105

Are the scenes making sense?

Where does it lag or slow down?

Don't rush this process, the film's story has to come through correctly and editing is where it happens. Your rough cut is your foundation, your skeleton. Once you get that done you can look ahead to the other elements you need in the film like CGI, your opening sequence credits, any animations, etc.

NOTE: Make sure you pick your best shots when your foundation is laid. You are building a house now, so everything has to start with your foundation. The goal is to get all the visuals, FX graphics/titles in place on the timeline. You are shooting for picture lock. Picture lock is the stage of editing when you are content with your shots and happy with all your edits. You have inserted your close-ups and medium shots, trimmed your edits, and tightened the timeline. Once in picture lock, it becomes time to move the film into Foley, sound effects, and music scoring.

Picture lock on the edit timeline actually means you lock the video tracks in your editor. You do this so you will not accidentally move, shift, or delete a scene in your edit. Picture lock may take three months or longer. As long as you are the editor that's fine. If you are paying someone by the hour, you want to avoid dragging picture lock on too long.

MUSIC FOR YOUR FILM

The next step is audio, music, and scoring. Designing the music score is yet another art form entirely. There can be no doubt by now that making a movie is a team game. It's best if you have someone who can compose music. You have to prepare the films for them.

At this point you can you give your composer a DVD of the picture lock, so he or she can create the emotional feeling of the film musically. Composers will have an idea by watching the scenes and the flow of the film. How much they actually score really depends and your budget, and how much music needs to be fit into each scene. You want cinematic scores throughout. You use music to create the emotion, drama, and suspense of the scene.

If you are on a tight budget then your next option is production music. Some great production music companies can be found online. Many are very inexpensive. In this scenario, this means you as the editor have to create the music score and sound design. You will have to know where to drop those cinematic scores and sound effects in throughout the film.

Creating a score for your film from production music is no easy task. It takes practice and a great deal of skill to feel where the music should start and stop to enhance the visuals in your scene. My advice is that you have someone who knows music. Perhaps even a local musician. Eventually you will acquire this skill if you are the director/editor.

NOTE: This is another element of production value. I am sure you have watched numerous indie films where the music made no sense in the shot. Scoring a film is not only done with your ears, it has to be done by feeling the mood of that scene.

I like to feel the music in the shot, to see if it fits with the mood of the scene. Since I spend so much time with the film as the director and then the editor, I get a feel for what will work and will not work.

Music and sound scores are not the only audio you will need to create for your film.

SOUND FX AND FOLEY

Sound effects and Foley fill the background audio tracks of your film. In a Hollywood film when you hear that shoe walking across the wood floor, it's not really done on location. It's done in the studio.

This is a big business. Hollywood hires a Foley effect artist to recreate effects in real time while watching that scene. In the low budget world, it is more time efficient and less costly to just find a drop in for that footstep effect. It would be nice to have three hundred dollars an hour to pay a Foley artist to create your effects, but let's be real.

NOTE: Hollywood filmmakers bring a film into the edit suite with no audio at all. They have a silent movie in front of them. They cut the film using any reference audio they recorded on location. The audio recorder on location is stripped away. They then bring the characters back into the studio to re read their lines. They re-sync the new dialogue tracks over the original footage, a process known as ADR.

This goes for the actual effects you may hear on screen. While some may be the real audio from the location, the Foley artist re-creates the sound effects in each scene. For our purposes and because we are working in the low budget world, you will not have the thousands of dollars it takes to have this done.

Now you know this is how they can control the sounds in the background of each shot. You will never hear crickets when cutting from one shot to another, or hear a church bell ringing in the wide shot and gone in the close-up. That church bell or those crickets were edited into the effect tracks after the scene was edited. All Foley work and sound effects are edited into the effect tracks later on, well after picture lock.

SOUND/AUDIO DESIGN

The sound design and audio design process is kept separate from the editing. In a big budget film, the picture lock is passed off to the audio studio for its work. In the low budget world, we just fire up another software package and continue to work.

Dialogue and Music tracks:

Every film—big budget or no budget—has to go through the same process for audio. The standard layout for audio is:

Dialogue tracks separate

Music (5.1 surround sound)

Music and effects tracks mixed

For the low budget filmmaker this can all be in the timeline. The process is done this way for a reason. For instance, say your distributor has interest from Russia to purchase your film. While English is spoken pretty much everywhere distributors would sell many more copies of your film in the countries' native language. They will take the dialogue tracks off your master hard drive and have the dialogue read by Russian actors. By having the tracks separate, your film still will have the proper music and effects as your original version. They simply hire an audio studio to lay in the new Russian dialogue tracks and mix them in with your effects and music tracks.

It is very smart to get location audio and room tone noise on location while you are there. Chances are you will use more production music and sound effects that are already made for you. In some scenes the more realistic the sounds are, the more credible the scene. If you are shooting at the beach, it's smart to have your sound crew record ten or fifteen minutes of beach sounds.

FINISH EDIT

Your final film elements will consist of completed:

Video tracks—All the scenes cut together

Master film edit—Complete feature film

Master trailer edit—Completed trailer

Dialogue tracks—The characters dialogue master file

Music tracks—The entire sound beds

Effect tracks—The sound FX and/or Foley tracks

All put together these will be the elements that make up your final master or final print as they used to say in the old days. You will be responsible for organizing these elements onto an external hard drive for shipment to the distributor. Once you have locked the picture and completed your music score and sound effects tracks you will move on to visual effects.

CGI—COMPUTER GENERATED IMAGERY

The one thing so many indie films lack is good CGI effects. It may just be a car on fire or a small explosion. CGI is an expensive and time-consuming process. For me, I knew shooting a sci-fi film would take a great deal of CGI effects. I had no choice but to take on the challenge of creating these effects on my edit system.

NOTE: I would never try it again. Your film will be compared to Avatar or Transformers. When your effects look amateurish, critics will slam your film. Unless you really have the budget to hire an animator, it is a very difficult thing to pull off. I would not say impossible, but difficult. If you are in a situation where you must have an effect, perhaps a small explosion or gunfire, some very good software packages can be used.

The website www.videocopilot.net is a professional source for tutorials and software to create some very good effects for your film. I purchased many of their tutorials.

Remember CGI effects take hours and hours of creation time.

NOTE: Don't even attempt to do CGI without Adobe After Effects.

I love Adobe After Effects. I've been using it now since its creation and know it very well. I could have never created some of the effects in our films without this powerful piece of software. This may be the most important purchase you make after purchasing your editing software. Sure, other programs exist for motion graphics, but AE to me is the best. The Video Copilot tutorials work in After Effects, and you can create some amazing effects.

NOTE: These effects take days and weeks of time to create and hours to render on your computer.

If your film needs to have these types of effects and you don't have the budget to hire someone then I would suggest this:

Purchase Adobe After Effects

Purchase the desired effect from Video Copilot

Learn the software (AE has a huge learning curve)

Set aside a couple of weeks for each effect.
If there is one redeeming feature in all this, a small piece of software can take your film to the next level. A company called GenArts makes a software package called Particle Illusion.

The site is www.wondertouch.com. The software is amazing and inexpensive. It lets you use hundreds of preset animations like fire, smoke, or rain and layer them over your footage. You may not have heard of the software, but you surely have seen it. The Sci-Fi Channel, Chiller, Fear Network all have movies that use this software package. Even TV shows like *Life After People, Smallville, JAG, 24* have Particle Illusion effects in them.

The software is designed for both MAC and PC. It will run in After Effects, Sony Vegas, or as standalone program. If you are adventurous and don't have the budget to hire a CGI artist then this is the software to get. Again, this is not easy software to perfect. With practice and time you can create some very real looking CGI.

COLOR GRADING AND COLORIZATION

Today when shooting HD, color grading is very popular when trying to make your HD video look more like film. Color correction will always be needed in your film because you want to make sure each shot has a similar look. When shooting with two different cameras, color correction is always necessary.

One of the best color correction and grading software packages available today is Red Giant software. Red Giant has the nicest people in the business and has been a sponsor of ours since our very first feature film. They provide professional packages for color correction and color grading as well as motion graphics. Their packages work on both MAC and PC.

Magic Bullet Looks is by far my favorite software and a powerful program. Many options exist for color grading. Magic Bullet Looks can make your film look like an entirely different movie. Magic Bullet also has a great green screen chroma key software. All their packages are available for Mac and PC.

NOTE: Color grading and color correction is another creative process that does take time to learn. You do this process last, once you are happy with your edited film and have locked the picture. This can also be the most fun part of the edit. Experiment with the different looks. There are some great pre-sets and each different look is customizable as well. The web page is www.redgiant.com. You will find great samples and tutorials on the site. I recommend you have this software in your editor. Some of the reasons to purchase from the website:

Share looks between apps. Share your Looks 2 presets between After Effects, Final Cut Pro, Premiere Pro, Vegas Pro, Motion, Media Composer, and Photoshop.

Start to finish. Design a look that can be used throughout post-production, from pre-vis to edit to the final master.

Huge library of presets. Professionally designed presets will kick start your video or film. Inspired by real-world projects and problems, and tested in commercial projects.

Tons of new tools. Now you get tools like video out preview, Colorista 3-Way wheels, ranged HSL, hue/lightness scope, hue/saturation scope, and Cosmo skin smoothing.

Works with any version. Full backward compatibility lets you easily work with Looks 1 and PhotoLooks presets.

MOVIE POSTER CREATION

More than likely you never even thought about the movie poster or the artwork for your film. You'll want to create a movie poster at this point. As with everything Hollywood does, some people just create movie posters and do nothing else. In the low budget world odds are you will have to work with a couple of your artistic and graphics friends to create a cool poster. The best way to design a poster is to look at other real movie posters, Hollywood movie posters. A good movie poster will tease the viewer into wanting to see your film. This doesn't always work though. Even in Hollywood with the big bucks some posters are just crap.

NOTE: Rachel created our movie posters. She literally spent hours on them, and it was good for her portfolio. The problem here is once you sell your film, all bets are off. No matter how hard you work on the artwork, distributors are going to end up changing your poster anyway. I'm not sure why that is, but it's happened to us four times now. I guarantee they will do it to you as well. They know what they want and like to package the entire scheme in certain colors. Once they own the film, they can do what they want with the artwork.

My advice is to create a temporary poster, something simple. You can use stills from the movie. Spending a lot of time creating a movie poster is not something you should do, especially if you plan to sell your film.

CUTTING THE PERFECT TRAILER

Once you have cut your film, you should know your footage by heart. It's now time to cut the official trailer. You have cut a couple different versions of the teaser on line and now you need to put the official trailer together. To me the trailer is the most important part of the editing and marketing process.

Your trailer sells your movie.

Your trailer will be the first thing people see as you market the film. You only get one shot to sell your film.

NOTE: Acquisition directors and distributors will gauge your film by your trailer. If they think your trailer sucks, they will never ask to see the film.

Hollywood spends massive amounts of money on one aspect of each film. Many companies only cut trailers, that's it. It's nice that Hollywood just throws money to get its problems solved. The indie just cannot do that. The best way to cut a sharp trailer is to watch hundreds of motion picture trailers.

What is a good trailer?

Is it attention getting and hard-hitting?

Are there strong dialogue bites?

Are there action scenes?

Analyze the trailers you view, dissect them to find out what is really going on. Cutting a trailer will take time. You will cut several versions until you find one that works for the film. Be meticulous with your trailer, it's the calling card for your film. If it's good distributors will know you have a good film. If you can't cut a ninety second trailer, then you certainly won't be able to cut a professional feature film.

Watch as many trailers as possible.

Know what is important in your film.

Find sound bites that are powerful.

Find a musical score that rises in tempo.

My trailers are always under one minute and thirty seconds. Shorter is much more effective, especially if you don't have named talent in your cast. When I teach classes on cutting a trailer, I see examples of trailers two, three, and sometimes four minutes long. That is unacceptable. You want to grab their attention, then get out. The whole idea here is to get people to want to see the movie. Leave them wanting more. Boring them with a long trailer will only hurt you.

NOTE: Never reveal your hook in a trailer. That may be the demon, the alien, or the hero's final act. You never reveal them. Yes, you can hint they are there, maybe from behind or in a reflection, but you never show your monster.

Tease, tease, tease. That is your goal.

Your trailer has to pop and make a statement in the first fifteen or twenty seconds. Make an unforgettable start.

CHAPTER 6

ORGANIZING YOUR FOOTAGE

Every distributor will ask you to organize all your files on one hard drive. The most important thing you can do is have your master files filed and organized in separate folders. If you begin this at the start of your edit all you will need to do is transfer them to the hard drive. This is part of the deliverable process.

NOTE: You will never see this drive again. Distributors will keep this drive in their studios for the duration of your contract. Do not send ORIGINAL MASTER FILES; these should all be digital copies of the originals.

As I noted earlier you never want to use re-manufactured or refurbished drives as your master edit drive. With that said, the time to purchase one of those drives is now when you need to make copies of the original files. If you can get a good re-manufactured drive cheaply enough use that to copy all your original files. You can send this drive to your distributor.

If you have a couple hundred bucks lying around then by all means purchase a new hard drive to send them. If you don't, a refurbished drive will suffice.

NOTE: Distributors are going to transfer your files from that drive to their edit servers or RAID system. After that, your hard drive is going to sit on a shelf in their storage rooms and will most likely never be fired up again.

I use this protocol. I always use refurbished drives to send to people who need an exact copy of my original files. Refurbished drives work fine to back up your master files. Just remember: Never use them for your original master files or as your edit drive.

You will want your drive to be organized and clean. That means each file is in its own folder and clearly marked.
VIDEO

AUDIO

MUSIC

ARTWORK

RELEASE FORMS

LEGAL

That's how I organize the deliverable hard drive. All distributors will have to do is open each folder to find what they need. Having said that, I have worked with some real dumb asses out west. No doubt, they smoke a lot of weed out there. I'm still not sure if it's the drugs, the sun, or if they just don't give a shit about their job.

Even with me taking the time to organize the deliverable hard drive and taking a screen capture of the files in it, they still could not find files they needed. There is no fixing stupidity. You may have to look at your master drive and call them to point out exactly where files are. It has happened to me every time.

The best thing at this point is that you are happy someone has purchased your film. Walk them through the hard drive to find the files they need. You are in the final lap. It won't be long now and you will be done handing the entire film to them. Be nice and make sure they get what they need.

DELIVERABLES

This is where your deliverable hard drive comes into play. Every distributor will have a list of deliverables. The list averages around twenty items you are responsible to send. You are responsible for these items both in delivery and financially.

If you want distributors to purchase your film, you have to give them what they want and when they want it in a timely fashion.

TRUE STORY:

I only knew about deliverables from my days working in television. I knew all video files had to meet certain specifications (specs) in order to be sent anywhere. I had never had to complete a list of deliverable items for a feature film. On our first film, all our negotiations with the distributor went through our attorney. The problem for me was that even after all the years in the production business I didn't know half of what I needed to know to deal with distributors. You will know even less. Television has one language and the movie business has another language all its own.

NOTE: Never go into negotiations with distributors thinking you know what they want. You don't. Every distributor is different and will ask for different elements.

Many know-it-all filmmakers in our area watch us sell movies and say, "Shit, I can do that." They can't. Having everything perfect for a distributor is a skill you can only learn by dealing with distributors. Little room exists for error. Give distributors what they want or they will just walk away from the deal.

I have found the easiest way to organize your film files is putting them in the proper folders as you go. Set up an external hard drive just for distributors. Label it with a big sticker and dedicate that drive just for them. When and (if) you sign a distribution deal you are only given thirty days to ship all the deliverables. By compiling and organizing the master files ahead of time, you stay one step ahead of the game.

Deliverables differ from distributor to distributor. The majority of distributors will want the following:

Finish master print in ProRes 422

Finished trailer in ProRes 422

Separate music tracks

Separate 5.1 or 7.1 music stems

Separate dialogue tracks

Separate the effects tracks

Two mastered DVDs

Original artwork

Location stills

Cast headshots

Cast release forms

Location release forms

Script copyright

Script option form

Script release form

Credit block

A music cue log sheet

The music rights release form

The film U.S. copyright

Poster art

Transcribed version of characters' dialogue

Errors and omission insurance

This is the basic list. The distributor you are dealing with may want more. Be prepared to have these elements ready. All these files should be placed on the master hard drive, organized and easy to find.

I know what you are saying now, "Wow, I never heard of some of this stuff." Hollywood not only makes the rules, it changes the rules when it feels like it. Imagine you don't know what some of these things are and every time you need a definition, your lawyer has to call the distributor.

It became a very costly lesson for me.

However, the benefit of this book is to save you thousands of dollars. Now you know you need to be prepared by having extra post-production money available when you get to editing.

TRUE STORY:

When I teach seminars I always hear rumbling when I tell filmmakers to always have money left over for post-production. Every indie filmmaker knows how hard it is to try to save money.

I knew a couple of filmmakers in New York who had wealthy parents. (Nice, huh?) They thought it would be cool to make a movie. They hit up their parents for money and in a couple of weeks they were ready to shoot a feature film. (It only takes months for us to raise money). I believe they got seventy-five thousand dollars for production. The real rub here is these guys never made a movie before. They hired all the local talent, had money to advertise, and got their film shot. I knew a few people in the cast, and after their shoot I was told it was the worst cluster fuck they had ever been a part of. None of them knew what they were doing. Here we have the typical know-it-all filmmaker wannabe with access to money, wanting to make a movie because it was fun. Even worse, they also thought they could edit their own film. I guess having rich parents gives you such a big safety net that you can gamble throughout the entire film. They gambled for sure, and lost. They could not get the film edited on their own. They had no clue how to start an edit. They thought they could just sit down and a movie would magically appear.

Having friends on the crew, I was told they had no money left for post-production and that's why they had to try to edit the film themselves. No experience at all, yet they thought they could edit a feature film. They had never thought to set money aside for editing. Well as pampered rich kids do, they just ended up going back to the well (mommy and daddy) and getting more money. To get the film edited it had cost them another seventy-five thousand dollars. However, it didn't end there. Once the film was done, they also decided it was best to hire a Hollywood sales agent, who charged them fifteen thousand dollars more.

We know firsthand the sales agent they used. We had met with him at AFM the year prior. Once he gave us his pep talk and how he could get our film marketed all over the world for a small fee, we politely left the room. You may or may not have the luxury of handing your film to a sales rep with a check for his services. I can tell you we never have. Knowing what I know now in this business, I would never waste that amount of money.

CREATING YOUR FILM SCREENER

Once you get to this point you are close to finishing the filmmaking process.

What everyone is going to want to see is your screener.

This is the time to actually send potential buyers the movie.

You won't just send them a copy of the film; that would be foolish and jeopardize all your hard work.

You will send them your screener. The screener is just copy of the film, set up with watermarks so your film cannot be stolen.

NOTE: The screener is watermarked for your protection. It's easily identifiable with your logo or other marking. Different variables of screeners will be accepted by some distributors.

Some screeners don't have credits.

Some screeners have full credits.

Some screeners don't have an intro.

Some screeners open up on the movie.

The screeners will contain the full movie, dialogue, and music and effects.

I have sent varying forms of screeners out to distributors. The most common screener I send now is the movie-only screener with watermark. No opening credits, no credit scroll. This is done for two reasons:

Not forcing the distributor to sit through a long opening and closing sequence.

Leaving the credits off should distributors want you to add their names.

You can only do this if you ask before sending your film.

NOTE: Remember—you never, never want to send out your screener without some kind of watermark or bug in the corner to discern that it is your work. In addition, you never want to send out your screener without permission of the distributor.

All unsolicited material ends up in the dumpster.

If no watermark or bug is in the corner, people can and will actually steal your movie. Some bootlegger in Beijing will be selling your film from his bicycle basket. Your screener needs to have a watermark or bug in the bottom right corner with your logo or saying this is the property of: _____.

Another great way to get your screener to distributors is posting your screener online. It has become acceptable practice these days. It will also save you time and money.

Vimeo is a professional media storage site that can host your screener to share privately. You can password protect your content and just send the link to prospective buyers. While this does work for some distributors, be prepared for some distributors to actually want a copy of the film on DVD. Many still want the DVD in their hand to watch on their home theatre system or in their office conference room.

NOTE: Not all distributors will watch your screener online. Don't get tripped up if a distributor says, "No we would like a DVD please."

ERROR & OMISSION POLICY

Error and omission insurance is what many distributors today want from filmmakers. Because this is a business, this is becoming a common requirement. Because we are a lawsuit happy society, distributors need to cover their asses.

NOTE: An error and omission insurance policy covers lawsuits challenging the use of copyrighted materials, plagiarism, defamation, invasion of privacy, ideas, and characters.

The concept of this policy is to defend any challenges to you or your film. An error and omission policy will cost around three thousand dollars. For the low budget filmmaker that's a big expense and one you were not expecting. Have your attorney ask your distributor up front if this is needed to complete your deal. If so, perhaps the distributor will work with you on how to pay for the policy.

NOTE: The E&O policy is not the same as production insurance. You will need both.

MPAA RATING
Some distributors can ask to have your film rated by the MPAA (Motion Picture Society of America). You are responsible for the cost, around six thousand dollars. As of this writing, most small, low budget films under a couple hundred thousand dollars are not required to have an MPAA rating. It really depends on where the distributor markets your film. I believe it will only be a matter of time before this may change. You will see indie films released today with no MPAA rating and that's a good thing for indie filmmakers. I'm

not sure how long this will last. Again, this is something your attorney can negotiate for you with your distributor.

What it comes down to at the end of your film is your attorney will be negotiating both the E&O policy and the MPAA rating. Both are potential deal breakers. If you have no money left by the time you finish editing, you certainly cannot absorb the additional nine or ten thousand dollars. Have your attorney negotiate with your distributor and see if you can get the distributor to pick up that tab and add it into the balance you will owe.

CHAPTER 7

ATTRACTING POTENTIAL DISTRIBUTORS

Let's step back and look at what we have accomplished to this point. Your film has been shot and edited. You are now at the selling stage of the game. You have made a list of distributors you want to contact. You put together a few people, your brother or sister, wife or husband to help you. As you begin to contact potential buyers, you will find yourself being asked the same two questions:

What is the budget? Who is in it?

Every distributor and acquisition director knows these are the two key selling points of any movie. Since we are shooting on a low budget odds are you have an unknown cast.

NOTE: Get prepared to answer this question every time you talk to someone about your film. This is a stock question you will be asked.

You know your trailer has to dazzle them.

Your movie screener is half as important as your trailer at this stage.

If you are lucky, distributors will watch your trailer. That will determine if they want to watch your screener.

Do your homework before you waste distributors' time. Know which distributors would buy your film. Know which distributors are looking for product.

In the low budget world, you are looking for a small boutique distributor or mini distributor. These are the types of distributors who look for films in a certain genre. These are the distributors willing to take a chance on a film with a no-name cast. Some of these distributors just release films domestically in the U.S. and others release films both domestically and worldwide.

Do your research; know a little bit about the distributor you are contacting:

What type of films does this company sell? Who makes up the company? Who is the acquisition director? How many films does this company purchase each year?

NOTE: The acquisition director at each distributor is the person in charge of buying new films for the company's catalogue. Contact that person and ask if the company is looking for new films to purchase.

NOTE: I always post our trailer on our website as well as on www.iftrailers.com. There, you can have people view your trailer. It also keeps track of how many people have watched your trailer and how popular it is. I believe our trailers are still in the top ten of the most viewed trailers. This helps in your marketing.

Acquisition directors are always looking for quality films. Make friendly contact by email. Email is the new way of doing business. Politely ask if they would be interested in viewing your trailer.

NOTE: This is why it is very important to have a link to your trailer online. Include that link in your email. If your trailer was edited correctly, acquisition directors will almost always ask to see your screener. If they don't ask to see your screener, don't bug them. Move on.

On a positive note, they are obviously interested if they reply. They also may reply and tell you your film is not a fit for their company. Keep that door open and thank them for their time. Ask if you could submit your next feature film for them to review.

You just created a distribution contact.

Their job is to find new films so they will more than likely encourage you to send them your next film. Save that information.

Finding a distributor is hard work; one thing you need to remember is very few films are purchased for distribution.

About six thousand indie feature films are made in the United States each year. According to the *Los Angeles Times* and the Hollywood Economist blog post, only 2 percent secure any type of distribution deal.

According to Mark Litwak, entertainment attorney, author, and professor, "Securing distribution is often more challenging than raising financing and producing the movie."

DON'T BE NAIVE

The days of distributors giving you a cash advance upfront are long gone. It just does not happen and it won't happen.

You will not get a chunk of cash upfront, period.

Get off your high horse and throw away the notion they are going to like your film so much they will offer you an advance.

You are responsible for the costs associated with getting your film packaged and to the distributor, not the other way around. Distributors are bombarded with films every day, especially today with the digital revolution and the ease of making feature films. Distributors are getting truckloads of shitty, unsellable films. If you are one of the *prima donna* filmmakers who thinks your film will be plucked out of the air over the six thousand other films, then you need to wake up to the real world.

NOTE: One of my favorite sayings and one I use when teaching is, "No one is going to open up their checkbook for you, you need to work for it." Exceptions exist to this rule, like the pampered New York filmmakers who got money from mommy and daddy, but overall you are in for a war. Know you have to fight for it, make it count. Be the best you can be.

Make sure your film stands out.

Make sure your trailer is world class.

Don't wait too long if offered a deal.

You already know thousands of films are out there. Not just from the U.S. but from around the world. I was told by one of our distributors who had just come back from Cannes that he had seen films from China made for ten thousand dollars that looked like Hollywood features. Great camera work, professional lighting, great acting, etc.

Don't get to cocky, the fact you were able to get a distributor interested in your film is a small battle won. This is a business and in this business, your film is the product.

TRUE STORY:

A couple of filmmakers in our area of New York and Boston had successful funding campaigns. While not huge budgets, they were able to raise two hundred and fifty thousand for one film and three hundred thousand for another. It takes money to make a movie. Always remember you cannot make a commercially sellable film with no money at all. Don't even try it.

NOTE: If you are trying to make a feature film for a couple thousand dollars in hopes a distributor will buy it, FORGET IT. The digital lab fees alone to prepare your film for release are a few thousand dollars.

I know these particular filmmakers, so I emailed them wishing them luck and offering help if they need it. I'm talking about more hobbyist filmmakers who thought it would be fun to make a movie. Not the hardcore filmmakers who do this for a living. These films were being shot only a couple of hours away from us so we kept up on their progress.

Both films completed principal photography. In addition, each filmmaker was able to hire a sales rep to help get the film to larger distributors.

NOTE: Sales reps take money up front. They don't do anything for nothing.

A few months passed and I heard nothing from either filmmaker. They entered their films in some small irrelevant film festivals and didn't even win those. Come to find out each film was offered a distribution deal from a small distributor; no advance money, just a basic distribution deal. Hearing the news, I emailed each to congratulate them. What I found out is that both of them had passed on the deal they were offered because they wanted to wait for a better deal. Remember when I said you jump on a deal as fast as you can or they will move on?

I have learned by now having that arrogant attitude goes nowhere in Hollywood. You are dealing with Hollywood.

These are the very people who invented arrogance.

If you are lucky enough to get any kind of offer, think it through. Needless to say, the two films that were made an offer are sitting in their respective bookcases; investors have not seen a dime of their money. It has been well over a year and no other offers have been made to them. The wait for a better deal concept is great if you are a Heisman Trophy winner coming out of college or a free agent coming off a World Series team.

In the indie film world, you only get one shot.

Waiting for a better deal to me means you better have a great attorney because you will be going to court to pay back investors.

NOTE: If a distributor makes you an offer, have your attorney get the contract and read it over. If you have done all your marketing around the same time, you should have a couple of offers on the table within a few weeks of each other. Get the distributors' offer in writing and have your attorney read it. You will have some time to evaluate the deals. Your attorney can also buy you some time.

NOTE: Do not be as arrogant as the two filmmakers I know and say no thanks to a distribution deal. I have seen this happen a few times now.

The odds are against you to begin with.

If you are fortunate enough to have someone interested in your film, take it seriously. You are certainly in the rare group of filmmakers who have the opportunity to have their films seen. You are close to becoming one of the 2 percent who actually gets a film sold.

QC-QUALITY CONTROL REPORT

The one single way Hollywood sorts out serious filmmakers from hobbyists is with protocol. Hollywood has a structured way of doing business, along with its own language and keywords.

The Quality Control Report or QC is one of those protocols you had better learn if you ever hope to sell your film overseas.

NOTE: I have battled with people from Boston to San Francisco about the QC report. Having success selling our films, I know firsthand we had to pass a QC report for each of them. This report is the key for films to be sold in foreign markets. People who have never sold a movie are in denial about the QC. They don't believe it exists. That may be for a very good reason. Many films never pass this QC report.

The QC not only exists, it was put in place so Hollywood could weed out the hobbyists from the professional filmmakers. If you have no professional experience editing, the odds are slim to none you will be able to pass this technical test.

The QC is made up of broadcast standards developed by the Germans to make sure a film meets both video and audio standards before it can be released in foreign territories.

The QC report looks at everything in your film: video, audio, edits, graphics, video levels, fades, titles, colors, artifacts, etc. It is a complete technical report of your film. I talked with the engineers at Fotokem Digital Lab in Burbank, CA. I had hired them to perform our QC report for *Back to the Beyond*. The head engineer told me 85 percent of films they service fail the QC report. This includes major Hollywood releases as well. The standards are quite high for a foreign release.

Your film will never be sold overseas without passing the quality control report.

The entire deliverable process is one big protocol test to see if you can follow the standards Hollywood has set up. This is how Hollywood separates those who have the skills to make commercial films from those who do not.

Personally, I have spent a good amount of time and money having our lawyer clarify what the distributor wants. The QC process is very confusing. It will also dictate the path of your films' exposure. By telling you this now, I hope to save you hundreds of dollars as well as hours of frustration and aggravation. Once you know what it is they want and use the same language they use you will have gained access to their system. You can use this information anytime you are dealing with distributors.

WHAT TO EXPECT

Nothing…expect nothing from your film.

Every filmmaker always thinks his film will be picked up by Lions Gate or Sony Pictures. That does not happen in real life. The odds are against you that you will even get your film sold. Expect nothing, and when someone does show interest in your film you will be pleasantly surprised and not crushed. If you go into this process making demands from the distributor, asking for things you are not going to get, or with a swelled head, your film will be sitting on the bookshelf collecting dust. Trust me, distributors are not sending a limo for you because you made a low budget horror movie. Distributors have to see some potential for making money with your film.

Let's look at what most likely will happen. The most common deal you are looking at today is called the standard distribution deal or net deal. Your film is on consignment while the distributor markets it around the world. The distributor will fund a few thousand dollars (the distributor loans you the money and recoups it off the top of the first sales). After recouping the fees, marketing costs and advertising you may split the profits 70 percent-30 percent or 50/50. This is the most common deal today.

If you have made it this far through my book, you know by now I don't bullshit. You will start your deal with a negative balance owed to your distributor. If your film is popular, you all make money. If your film flops, you will not see a dime.

All distributors will be open-minded about you helping to sell your film. They are all for you setting up screenings or events surrounding your film as long as it brings in money. Buzz Remde at R-Squared Films is one of the most honest, straight shooters around. He will tell you what he thinks your film can make and where it will sell. You want a distributor who will tell it like it is.

Don't go out and buy that motor home or cabin on the lake.

This is not going to be your ticket to millions. Just because you signed a distribution deal does not mean you will get royalty checks every six months. The average low budget film will take two years to recoup money, if it makes money at all. We received our first royalty check some sixteen months after the release of *Back to the Beyond*. I didn't hold my breath waiting.
NOTE: Distributors will never tell you how much your film is worth. Having great relationships with our distributors, I was able to get some rough data on the actual value of a low budget, indie movie with no-name actors. Distributors have a scale they use. These are ballpark numbers and change according to the market.

A feature film that passes the QC with a no-name cast has a return value of $10K-$70K. Today in the digital world it's a buyer's market. Thousands of films are being made, so distributors can pick and choose. Rarely will an indie film with a no-name cast make more than $50,000.

Again, don't count on that being the case. That is what the distributor is looking to get as a return from your film.

Netflix is no longer indie friendly.

We were able to get our first film picked up by Netflix and Blockbuster. Since that time Netflix has changed its rules on accepting indie films. Netflix no longer supports the independent filmmaker and will not accept indie films unless you have worldwide distribution and a named actor or actress in your movie. Typical corporate BS. The one place indie filmmakers could expect to get exposure is Netflix. It now no longer wants their films. My hope is that with all the new digital channels and networks someone will stand up and accept all the great indie films and surpass Netflix as the number one streaming service.

DON'T GET DISCOURAGED

You worked hard to make your movie, you spent months of your life to get this film done, and you never quit. Great, you still need to work harder to get people to see it.

Don't get discouraged when people don't want to see your screener. As I said previously, never add pressure to an acquisition director or distributor. It's like a job interview. Distributors have to consider other factors before purchasing the rights to a film. Let distributors review your film on their time, give them a couple weeks then follow up by email. The last thing you want is to be the pain in the ass filmmaker who won't leave them alone.

Be polite and not pushy. Become friendly with their secretary. If they pass on your film, you still want to keep their email for your next project.

If you just entered the low budget filmmaking world then this kind of rejection is what you will face on a daily basis. If you have been in this business, you know rejection is a way of life; you suck it up and just move on. I told you before this is not a business for the weak or timid.

VARIOUS DISTRIBUTION WINDOWS

Distribution deals have film distribution windows. How it works is distributors roll out your film in waves.

Theatrical release (if you are really lucky)

Blu-Ray or DVD release

VOD (video on demand) and online streaming

Cable TV and satellite

That's basically what they are going to look at and how they will release your movie.

Keep in mind that only 2 percent of all movies get any kind of distribution deal. Today with HD equipment becoming cheaper and cheaper, the odds are getting slimmer and slimmer indie filmmakers will be able to sell their films with all the competition. Be proud of what you accomplished.

If you do sell your film you will be both respected and hated. Yes, hated by fellow filmmakers who are jealous of what you are doing. One of the biggest comments you will hear and I cannot tell you how many times people have said they heard other filmmakers say, "If they can do it, then I can do it."

If they could sell their films they would have, right? Maybe if they purchase this book they have a shot now. It comes from frustration and jealousy, I'm sure. Be prepared for the cold shoulder, but always keep your head up.

JUST FOLLOW YOUR HEART

If you are like me, you have known for quite some time you want to make movies. Since the age of thirteen, I always knew I wanted to make movies. Follow your heart and stay focused on your dream. I can tell you first hand it won't be easy at all. There will be days you will hate doing this art. There will be setbacks, illnesses, frustration, and stress. The only people who attain any kind of success in this business are the ones who adopt the motto, never quit. Thousands of people before you had the same dream but didn't posses the heart to follow through.

Filmmaking is not only an art; it's a test of your will.

If you have the dedication and the drive to make movies, no doubt you can succeed. A friend encouraged me early on. Even though he's a PC guy, Kerry Knowlton, a director, ex-pro wrestler and someone I bounced ideas off during my first film, came up with some great advice. Kerry told me, "Just get your film made. You have won the battle by just getting it made. Keep working hard and it will sell." I pass this same advice on to you. I thank you for reading this book and hope you have a long and successful journey doing what you like to do.

Glossary

1080/24p: The standardized international high definition format having a sampling structure of 1920 (H) x 1080(V) and operating at 24-frames/second progressively scanned.

1080/60i: The standardized international high definition format having a sampling structure of 1920(H) x 1080(V) and operating in interlaced scan mode at 60-fields/second.

1280x720: Refers to the high definition sampling structure of 1280(H) x 720(V). All 1280x720 images are scanned progressively.

1920x1080: Refers to the high definition sampling structure of 1920(H) x 1080(V). 1920x1080 images can be scanned either interlaced or progressive.

23.98 or 23.976: A video frame rate of 23.976 (truncated to 23.98) frames/second. This is deliberately offset from 24 frames so that a simple 3:2 process will produce the standard 59.94-fields/second interlaced video.

24PsF: Term used to describe a 24 (23.98) frame progressive video that divides the video in segments of odd and even lines for transmission and storage and display.

2K: A film image scanned into a computer file at a resolution of 2048 horizontal pixels per line.

30p: 30 full-frames/second digital video progressively captured. Often referred to as 29.97p.

3:2 Pulldown: The process used to convert 24-frame/second film or 24p video into 54.94i video. The 3:2 process consists of two (2) parts the pulldown and the 3:2 cadence. The pulldown process is the slowing of the film or video to 23.976-frames/second. The 3:2 cadence is created by taking one (1) frame of the 24-frame source and filling three (3) of the 59.94 fields.

4:2:2: A commonly used term for component digital video format. The numeral 4:2:2 denotes the ratio of the sampling frequencies of the single luminance channel to the two color difference channels. For every four- (4) luminance samples, two (2) samples of each color channel exist.

4:4:4: A sampling ratio that has equal amounts of luminance and both chrominance channels. Also known as CCIR-6601.

4K: A film image scanned into a computer file at a resolution of 4096 horizontal pixels per line. 4K is considered to be the full-resolution scan of 35mm film.

5.1 Audio: An arrangement of five (5) audio channels (left; center; right; left-surround; right-surround) and one (1) sub-woofer channel.

16X9: A wide-screen format in which the aspect ratio of the screen is 16 units wide by 9 units high as opposed to the 4x3 of normal television.

24P: A video picture in interlaced, i.e. first all the odd numbered fields are scanned then all the even ones. There are 60 fields in one frame of video and 30 frames per second. A progressive scan scans the fields in order, i.e. 1,2,3,4, etc. It gives more of a film-like look.

59.94 Fields/Second: The field rate of NTSC color television.

60 Fields/Second: The field rate of SMPTE HDEP standard.

720/60p: Refers to the high definition format of a sampling structure of 1280(H) x 720(V) and operating at 60-frames/second progressively scanned.

A/B Roll: Creates fades, wipes, and other transitions from one video source to another.

A to D Converter: An electronic device used at the input of digital audio equipment to convert analog signals to digital values.

Action Safe Area: The area of a television picture visible on consumer television sets.

ADR: Automatic Dialogue Replacement. Recording/re-recording dialogue where the production sound is unstable or obscured.

AES/EBU: Informal name for a digital audio standard established by the Audio Engineering Society & European Broadcast Union. It is the transmission of two (2) channels of digital audio data on a single twisted-pair cable using 3-pin (XLR).

AGC: An acronym for automatic gain control. It is the circuitry used to ensure output signals are maintained at constant levels despite widely varying input signals.

Aliasing: Defects or distortions in a television picture due to sampling limitations. Defects are commonly seen as jagged edges or diagonal lines and a pulsing/brightening in picture detail.

Alpha Channel: Additional channel that saves the relative transparency value additionally to the color information. The alpha channel is an additional channel that saves the relative transparency value additionally to the color information. Thanks to the alpha values the layering of media objects on top of each other are facilitated. In the common four-digit digital-sampling structure like 4:2:2:4, the alpha channel is represented by the last digit.

Analog: A continuous electrical signal that carries information in the form of various physical values such as amplitude or frequency modulation. Voltage or current rather than a set of digital numbers, represents a pixel.

Anamorphic: A film image horizontally compressed by a special lens to fit the width of a standard academy ratio film frame then expanded during projection to its normal width and appearance on the screen. The vertical axis is not disturbed during this process.

Answer Print: The first film print combining picture and sound in release form offered by the film-processing laboratory to the producer for acceptance.

API: An acronym for application program interface. Using this source code interface, a programmer can make requests of the operating system or another application.

Array: When storing information on multiple devices of data storage, it is defined as an array.

Artifacts: Refers to video blemishes, noise, or any physical interruption of the video image.

Aspect Ratio: The ratio of the width of a picture to the height.

Asstalker: Constant liar, people who promise but never deliver.

Assemble Edit: Building videotape in which a series of clips are placed in order, one after another.

Audio Clip: In a non-linear editing environment a clip indicates data of either video or audio that has been clipped out (copied) from a larger environment such as a reel or videotape.

Auto Assembly: Automatic combining of edits on videotape conforming to a prepared edit decision list (EDL) with little or no human involvement.

Backup: Copying files or databases so they will be preserved.

Bandwidth: Data throughput, meaning the amount of data sent. The term describes the amount of information that can be transmitted over a wire, line or method of linking communication devices. Therefore, it defines the range of transmission frequencies a network can use. The greater the bandwidth is, the larger the amount of information that can be transferred over that network.

Batch Capture: Combining your video capture card with deck control so that you define the in and out points first, then capture only the footage you want.

Bin: On non-linear editing systems the bin is an organization tool for one or more film scenes.

Bit: Short for binary digit. The smallest piece if binary digital data and is represented by either a 1 or a 0. Numbers of bits are used in digital video as a representation of signal quality (i.e. an 8-bit signal can have 256 levels from black to white while a 10-bit signal can have 1024 levels).

Bit Depth: The bit depth is an indication of the color depth that a pixel in a digital image may have. For example, when the image is available in 8 bit, each pixel in the image will provide one of 256 colors (28); when the image is in 10 bit, up to 1024 colors (210) are available.

Black Burst: A composite video signal consisting of all horizontal & vertical synchronization information. It is typically used as the house reference synchronization signal in television facilities.

BMP: An abbreviation for bitmap, i.e. the Windows bitmap format. An image file format that can be used for video clips.

BNC: An acronym for British naval connector. A cable connector used exclusively in television.

Bottom Feeder: Individuals who constantly ride your coat tail. People who copy your actions.

Breakout Box: A box to be connected to a computer system to provide further connections. In a digital video environment, a breakout box may provide further connections for the video system, for example, to in- or output audio or video.

Breakout Cable: At hardware (e.g. a video system) input/output connections that are usually distributed over several standardized connectors can be combined and offered via a single connector for the sake of space.

Broadcast Quality: Footage that meets the high technical standards for broadcast or cablecast. Quality that does not meet this standard is referred to as reference quality.

Burn-in: Burn-in means to superimpose certain information on another image. With such a feature, you can provide each image with individual information such as timecode, frame or keycode data or comments.

Bus: A bus is a group of data, control, and/or addressing lines that extend from device to device and act as a conduit for signals. A bus is often shared by several devices.

Byte: A byte consists of 8-bits or 10-bits.

Cache: Cache is an especially fast memory. It is a collection of duplicated data values stored in a memory.

Camera Report: The form used to identify what is on each exposed camera roll and any special printing or transfer instructions.

Capture: Process of feeding media material from outside sources into a computer. Capturing media from an outside source requires special hardware, the video capture card. Special software is needed too, when capturing video of what is displayed on the computer screen.

Capture Rate: A term used to describe the number of times/second a picture is taken or captured in an imaging system. In a progressive system, the capture rate is equal to the frame rate. In an interlaced system, the capture rate is double the frame rate. This is because at each capture interval only one (1) field (a half resolution image) is acquired. It takes two (2) fields to make a complete frame.

CG: An acronym for computer graphics. Usually it stands for images either partially or completely created at a computer workstation. However, in the field of digital video CG-matrices are used to color convert images from the YUV color space (the color space of television signals) to the RGB color space (the color space used on computers) and vice versa.

Check Print: First film print used to check color corrections.

Chromakeying/Chromakeyer: Overlaying one video signal over another is defined as chromakeying. The areas of overlay must be defined by a specific range of color or chrominance, depending on the foreground signal. The chrominance must have sufficient bandwidth or resolution. Chromakeying is also called blue screen or green screen, depending on the color being replaced.

Chrominance: The portion of the video signal that contain color information.

Client: A computer system that wants to access a service—sometimes a remote one—on another computer is called a client. Typically, this happens within a network.

CMYK: An acronym for cyan; magenta; yellow; black. It is the designation for the subtractive color system used in pigment printers.

Coding: Ink stamping or burning numbers into the edges of work print and work track to mark sync points. It is done with a coding machine.

Color Bars: A video test signal widely used for system and monitor set-up. The test signal typically contains eight (8) basic colors (white; yellow; cyan; magenta; blue; black) and is used to check chrominance functions of color television systems.

Color-Correction: Alteration of the tonal values of colored objects or images.

Color Space: This term describes the color range between specified references. Normally, references in television are quoted in the following way: RGB, Y, R-Y, B-Y, YIQ, YUV and hue saturation and luminance (HSL), and XYZ.

Color Temperature: A concept formulated for the purpose of reference and standardization of color light sources. The color temperature is expressed in degrees centigrade beginning at absolute zero (Kelvin scale).

Component: Component signal keeps luminance and chrominance separate. It provides better picture quality.

Component Analog: The unencoded output of a camera, videotape, etc., consisting of three (3) primary color signals, i.e. red, green & blue (RGB), that together convey all necessary picture information.

Component Digital: A digital representation of a component analog signal set, most often Y, B-Y, R-Y.

Composite: Composite combines luminance and chrominance. It is usually less expensive than component.

Composite Analog: An encoded video signal, such as NTSC or PAL video that includes horizontal and vertical synchronization information.

Composite Digital: A digitally encoded video signal, such as NTSC or PAL video that includes horizontal and vertical synchronization information.

Composite Print: A film print incorporating picture and sound elements on the same strip of film.

Compositing: Layering multiple pictures on top of each other. Used primarily for special effects.

Compress: The process of converting video and audio data into a more compact form for storage or transmission. Compression Ratio: A value that indicates by what factor an image file has been reduced after compression. The higher the ratio the greater the compression.

Conforming: To prepare a complete version of your project for viewing or playing out by conforming it. The conformed version might either be an intermediate working version or the final cut.

Content Management System (CMS): A CMS will help its users administrate large amounts of content. When using a large body of documents or multimedia or image resources a CMS will help its users administrating this kind of content.

Cropping: A rectangular cutting of image edges. By cropping, you remove a part of your image. For example, to receive a letterbox effect (black borders at the top and bottom). As opposed to zoom and pan where you can create a similar effect, the remaining image is normally not scaled back to the size of the video format but remains in its original size.

Cursor: The vertical bar that represents an exact point in an active (text) object.

Cut: Instant change between two sources of video, also called hard cut. However, you can also create cuts or cutting points by simply dividing a video clip at a certain position.

Cut List: A cut list is usually provided as a file and used to determine a sequence of video and audio clips. It describes a timeline with video and audio clips via timecode data of succeeding in- and outpoints. Cut lists may also contain information about transitions between clips (hard cut or wipe) and exist in various different not standardized formats. See also EDL and Timeline.

DA: An acronym for distribution amplifier. A device used to multiply a video signal so the signal stays constant throughout a number of devices.

DA-88: A Tascam-brand eight-track digital audiotape machine using the 8 mm video format.

Dailies: Picture and sound work-prints of a day's shooting without regard to color-balance. Referred to as rushes in England. They are produced so the best takes can be selected.

Direct Attached Storage (DAS): A storage unit directly attached to the device recording the data.

DAT: An acronym for digital audio tape, a consumer digital audio recording and playback system with a signal quality surpassing the compact disc (CD).

DCP: An abbreviation for digital cinema package. A DCP is a collection of digital files used to store, organize, and convey Digital Cinema image, audio, and data streams. These include MXF, XML, and JPEG2000 files. SMPTE standards are used to conform various vendors, producers and distributors.

D-Cinema: Digital Cinema. It encompasses digital distribution and projection of digital cinematic material.

Decibel (dB): A unit of measure used to represent audio transmission levels, gains, or losses. It describes the smallest perceptible change in audio level.

Decoder: A device used to recover component signals from a composite (encoded) source.

Decompression: When expanding a compressed file back into its original form it is uncompressed (or decompressed).

Defragmentation: Storing and deleting data on a storage medium such as a hard disk will cause in time a fragmentation of data on the storage. At that point, the information is no longer stored as a large block in one place but scattered all over the storage. Though one will hardly experience this as a problem when working with a computer, when dealing with digital video it is of special importance: Then the data on the storage should be optimally aligned to be more suited for real-time operations. To achieve this you have to apply a defragmentation at regular intervals to the storage, which will physically align the data properly on the storage. For this, DVS developed a special defragmenter that even observes video clips consisting of individual image files: The files belonging to clips will be aligned in blocks, thus truly facilitating real-time processes.

Depth of Field: A term used to describe the areas of a picture both in front and behind the main focus point that remains in focus.

Digitizing: The act of taking analog audio and/or video and converting it to digital form.

Digital Intermediate (DI): A digital intermediate is the result of the process of shooting in high definition or shooting on film followed by scanning to film quality data files, editing the project in high definition and applying the creative process of color correction and color treatment to the completed master. This digital intermediate (DI) then becomes the master for video, DVD or for theatrical output by transferring this data master back to film.

Digital Television (DTV): The transmitting of a broadcast signal that consists of digital data.

Director's Cut: A rough-cut created by the director once the editor's cut is complete.

Disk Mirror: A disk mirror is a complete copy of data that resides on one physical disk to another physical disk. It doubles the data storage requirement when implemented. Also known as RAID Level 1.

Disk Striping: Disk striping is a technique used for spreading data over multiple disk drives. Disk striping speeds-up operations that retrieve data from disk storage.

Dissolve: A certain style of transition where one clip blends into the next. Most common are dissolve rates from a half-second to two seconds.

Down-Conversion: The process of converting high-resolution video to lower-resolution video.

DP: The director of photography.

Drift: When an element does not keep a steady pace during playback. Usually caused when there is no timecode to lock to or when the record machine power supply is faulty. It can also refer to a color-correction setting on a telecine, which has changed over time due to light-tube burn.

Driver: A program interacting with a special kind of software or particular device. The driver has special knowledge of the device or particular software interface that programs using the driver do not have.

Drop Frames: Frames/image files that cannot be read from or written to a storage device during a real-time operation have to be dropped, i.e. they will be omitted during a play-out or record. A drop can be caused by all kinds of reasons. For example, a fragmented video storage where data is physically scattered over the hard disk so it takes too long to read it in time.

Douche-Waffle: A person who always finds a way to screw up your plans.

DV: A video tape format designed primarily for the consumer market that records a 4:1:1 standard definition signal with a 5:1 compression ratio for a total bit-rate of 25Mb/second. DV cassettes come in two (2) sizes standard and mini.

DVI: An acronym for digital visual interface. It is a video standard interface that will maximize the visual quality of digital display devices (e.g. computer displays, LCD panels, digital projectors and more). It is especially suited for uncompressed digital video data.

DVCPro HD: A high definition format developed by Panasonic. It uses 1-inch wide tape stock and records 22:11:11 8-bit HD video.

DVD: An acronym for digital versatile disk. It is the same size as a compact disk (CD) but with a storage capacity up to 17 Gbytes.

EDL: An acronym for edit decision list. A list of a video production's edit points. It is a record of all edit decisions made for a program in the form of a printed copy, paper tape or floppy disk file, which is used to assemble the project at a later date.

Edge Crop: A technique whereby just the center portions of a wide aspect ratio format are viewable.

Edge Numbers: Sequential numbers printed along the edge of a filmstrip by the manufacturer which allow frames to be easily identified either by human or machine.

Effect: To add an image or sound to an original piece of film data not there before. It will make the original piece more interesting. Process is mostly carried out electronically.

Embedded: Embedded usually stands for embedded audio in video (AIV). Via SDI or HD-SDI up to 16 channels of audio (AES/EBU) can be transmitted. While this is the easiest way to transmit audio together with video, working on audio alone is normally not possible with this connection. See also AES/EBU and AIV.

Ethernet: A network technology for data transmission. A star-topology with twisted pair wiring is the most popular form. Common data rates are 10 Mbit/sec (Ethernet, 10 Base-T), 100 Mbit/sec (Fast Ethernet,100 Base-T), 1000 Mbit/sec (Gigabit Ethernet, 1000 Base-T) and 10,000 Mbit/sec (10 Gigabit Ethernet).

Fade: Different kinds of transitions, e.g. cross-fade. Fade-in: A transition from a blank screen to an image. A fade-out is also called fade to black. This describes the process of a transition from an image to a blank (usually black) screen.

Fader: A console control, which allows an operator to perform manual dissolves, fades and wipes.

FAT: FAT is an acronym for file allocation table. It is a table the system builds on a hard disk to keep track of what sectors are bad, are in use and by what file and in what sequence. Damage to the FAT is catastrophic.

Fibre Channel: A communications protocol designed to meet the requirements related to the demand for high performance data transfer. It supports data transmission and framing protocols for SCSI, HIPPI, Ethernet, Internet Protocol (IP) & ATM.

Field: A field is a half of a video frame; either odd or even scan lines.

Filter: A filter is a computer software module used to process digital video for adding special effects to a program.

File System: When storing and organizing computer files and their accompanying metadata, a popular method to use is a file system. A file system might possibly have a storage device (e.g. hard disk) and then maintaining the physical location of the files is of importance. The file system will translate the file name used by the user to the physical address on the storage device. Another option is the file system grants access to data on a file server then acting as clients for a network protocol. File systems might be virtual, too, and then only exist as an access method for virtual data.

Finalizing: The process used to finish a video sequence. On a video system, it is a process that generates a new clip from the project's timeline while the original material is not touched or altered. It saves the contents of the timeline in a freely selectable file and video/audio format to a new location, thereby applying all effects and cutting away material that is not needed.

Finishing: The complete process after fine-tuning the cutting and applying primary color corrections, such as applying secondary color corrections and titling.

FireWire: A special high-speed bus standard capable of more than 100 Mbits/second sustained data rate. Also known as IEEE P1394.

Flash Frames: White frames between frames with images on them. In video, these are mistimings in the EDL or editing that leave empty frames between cuts.

Flip-Flop: An effect on a video system where the video images are mirrored either horizontally (flip) or vertically (flop). See also Effect.

Flying Head: A video head that engages when a video deck is on pause, providing a clear still-frame image.

FMV: An abbreviation for full motion video. Video that plays at 30 fps (NTSC) or 25 fps (PAL).

Foley: Background sounds added during audio sweetening to heighten realism.

Forced Display: A DVD feature that forces the display of a sub-picture regardless of the wishes of the user.

Format: (1) The size, resolution, aspect ratio, color space, bit depth, format rate, etc. for a given image. (2) The file format for a given image. (3) The physical medium (such as film, video, etc.) used to capture or display an image sequence.

FPS: An abbreviation for frames per second.

Frame: A frame consists of all the information required for a complete picture. Each video frame has 2 interlaced fields. In the NTSC system, there are 525 interlaced horizontal lines of picture information in 29.97 frames per second. In the PAL system, there are 625 interlaced horizontal lines of picture information in 25 frames per second.

Frame Rate: Used to describe the number of times per second a complete picture is updated in an imaging system. FTP: An acronym for file transfer protocol. It allows users to transfer files over a TCP/IP network.

Full-Field: A complete video image consisting of 2 fields per video frame.

Gain: The increase or decrease in the strength of an electronic signal.

Genlock: The process of locking both the sync and burst of one signal to the burst and sync of another signal thus making the two signals synchronous.

Ghosting: Artifacts typically caused by signal leakage (crosstalk) between the two eyes. A secondary ghost image can be seen. Several possible causes can introduce the problem during acquisition, post-production and display. One reason can be high contrast levels between an object and its background.

Gigabyte: A digital storage capacity equivalent to one-billion bytes.

GPI: An acronym for general-purpose interface. This interface is mostly used in broadcast and post-production equipment. Some of these external devices do not have the ability to be directly controlled by the editor. In this case, the

GPI signal is used to synchronously start this equipment at the same time.

Gray Scale: A chart with varying shades of gray which is photographed during production and used by the film processing lab to color correct film.

GUI: An acronym for graphical user interface. An interactive graphic displayed on a screen, being a means of operating software.

HD: An acronym for high definition. It is frequently used to abbreviate HDEP and HDTV.

HD-SDI: An acronym for high definition serial digital interface. Describes the transmission of digital video in HDTV (1920)

HD Cam: A high definition videotape format developed by Sony Electronics. It utilizes 1/2-inch wide tape stock and a compression ratio of 2.7:1 at 440Mb/second.

HDTV: Collective term for television and video formats of a resolution higher than standard TV, with various proposals and standards. The most common formats standardized by SMPTE and others have 1280 x 720 pixels and 1920 x 1080 pixels Besides television applications, the HDTV equipment is also used in production and post-production of feature films. Both formats can be used with frame rates from 23.976 up to 60 frames per second. While 1920 x 1080 typically is used with interlaced scanning, in this case with a maximum frame rate of 30 fps, 1280 x 720 is always progressive but with frame rates up to 60 fps, i.e. the frame rate of the 1280 x 720 format is normally twice the frame rate of the 1920 x 1080 format.

Head and Tail: Video or audio material at the beginning (head) or end (tail) of a clip that is available on the storage of a non-linear editing system but not used nor visible in the timeline due to an adjustment (trimming) of the clip's in or out point. Clips recorded with heads and/or tails offer reserves in their content for further corrections during editing.

High Definition Image: 1920 x 1080

Hold: An interpolation setting that maintains settings from one key frame until the next key frame and uses only one frame to jump to the next setting.

Host: A host is a parent or base system accessing a RAID array for the purpose of data storage. Any system connected to a network.

HSDL: An acronym for high-speed data link. It is used to transmit and receive uncompressed 2K or 4K images. It is an expansion of the dual-link HD-SDI interface offering an easy way at a production site to share such data. With HSDL, the frame rate has to be reduced to 15 to 20 fps for 2K or even 5 fps for 4K images. See also Frame Rate, HD-SDI, SDI, and dual link.

Insert Edit: Placing a section of a source clip in the time line with the media currently to the right of the insert point is moved farther to the right to accommodate the new clip.

Interface: A boundary between adjacent components, circuits, or systems that enables the devices to exchange information.

Interlace: Technique for increasing picture repetition rate without increasing bandwidth by dividing a frame into separate fields.

Interlaced: A display system in which two (2) interleaved fields are used to create one (1) frame. The number of field lines is equal to one-half of the frame lines. Interlacing fields allows the level of light on a screen to be more constant thus reducing flicker.

Interlock: A system that electronically links a projector with a sound recorder.

Internegative: A duplicating film stock that turns into negative when printed from a positive print. It is used as a source for interpositive prints.

IP: An acronym for Internet protocol. The network layer protocol for the Internet protocol suite.

I/O: This stands for input/output. This term is used in situations where data is transferred to and/or from a system or devices.

Jog/Shuttle: To move through a clip or sequence frame by frame with different speeds forward or backward.

Jogging: Single frame forward or backward movement on videotape.

JPEG: An acronym for joint photographic expert group, a compression technique for still images and motion video. It is not as effective as MPEG, which is optimized for motion video.

Jump Cut: Transition between two scenes which makes the subject appear to jump. A cutaway shot remedies this alignment situation.

Kelvin: A system or scale for measuring temperature. Absolute zero is 0° Kelvin or -273° C. The color of white light is expressed in degrees Kelvin.

Key: A signal that can electronically cut a hole in a video picture to allow the insertion of other elements.

Key Channel: Also called alpha channel. A black-and-white video signal that can be added to the existing channels of a video signal (YUV[A] or RGB[A]). Normally used to determine parts of a video image that can be replaced by other content.

Layback: Transferring the finished audio track back to the master video tape.

LCD: An acronym for liquid crystal display. A text/graphics display technology where minute electrical currents change selected parts of the display screen.

Letterbox: When a wide-screen image is projected onto a television screen, a space is left on the top and bottom of the screen.

Letterbox Format: A technique for displaying a wide aspect ratio format on a narrower aspect ratio screen.

Locked: A video system is considered to be locked when the receiver is producing horizontal syncs that are in time with the transmitter.

Locked Cut/Locked Picture: The final version of a show after all the changes have been incorporated.
Log: At the beginning of an editing process, the information about source material is entered into bins, i.e. it is logged. Logging can either be done automatically or manually, before capturing or while capturing material.

Loop: Playing back a section of a timeline or clip again and again.

Luminance: The portion of the video signal that contains the brightness information for the picture, without color information. A black and white picture contains luminance information only.

Mac OS: Operating system of Apple Macintosh computers.

Mapping: A technique for taking 2D images and applying it as a surface onto a 3D object.

Matte: The black bars found at the top and bottom of the picture when a widescreen format is projected on a television set.

MB: Megabyte. A standard unit for measuring the information storage capacity of disks and memory. 1,000 kilobytes equals one (1) Megabyte.

Mbps, Mb/s: An abbreviation for megabits per second. A measurement of data transfer speed equivalent to one-million bits per second.

Media Management: Managing media means moving and storing digital content assets in a safe way, while managing requests for duplicates.

Memory: A computer's internal storage area. It is either data storage that comes in the form of chips or data that exists on tapes or disks. Also, the term memory is used as shorthand for physical memory.

MHz: An abbreviation for megahertz. A measurement of frequency equivalent to one-million hertz.

Mixing: Combining all sound tracks onto a single master track.

MPEG: An acronym for moving picture experts group. Standards designed for the handling of highly compressed moving images in real-time.

Multi-Channel: A term describes the number of channels (multiple) of audio or video.

Native Material: Certain video systems such as digital disk recorders or VTRs can only be configured to accept one video format a time. With VTRs, the dependence on a definite video format is determined by the format of the used tape. With digital disk recorders, it may depend on the format of the recorder's storage. This is then called the native material or the material native to the device.

NLE: This term describes a form of the editing process. Here, the recording medium is not a tape, therefore, editing can be performed in a non-linear manner, i.e. the editor is independent of the sequence of the program. NLE has the advantage of editing with quick access to source clips and record space (e.g. on computer disks). Moreover, it removes the need of winding and pre-rolling of VTR operations and hence speeds up work. Even greater speed and flexibility are possible when real-time random access to any frame (true random access) is applied. The term NLE is mostly used when discussing offline editing systems storing highly compressed images, but increasingly online non-linear systems are available as well. Nowadays quite a range of systems claim online quality with video compression. Still, prospective users have to judge the suitability of the results for their application and bear in mind that for transmission/ distribution the signals will be decompressed and re-compressed again.

Noise Reduction: Electronic reduction of observable grain in the picture.

Non-Drop Frame: System of timecode that retains all frame numbers in chronological order.
Non-Linear Editing: See NLE above.

NTFS: Acronym for Microsoft Window's new technology file system. It is a file system from Windows, used for storing and retrieving files. It allows data security on fixed and removable disks.

NTSC: NTSC is an acronym for national television system committee. It is the standard for broadcast color television in the United States, Canada, Central America and Japan. NTSC image format is 4x3 aspect ratio; 525 horizontal lines; 60 Hz and 4 MHz bandwidth with a total 6 MHz video

Numb: Individuals who just don't get it. Clueless to the outside world.

Off-Line Editing: Editing to produce an edit decision list (EDL) which is used to assemble the program at a later date.

On-Line Editing: Editing done to produce a finished program master.

Operating System: Every computer needs a base program, the so-called operating system that manages the computer and grants control of various functions. Common examples are MS DOS and Windows(R) for PCs, Mac OS for Apple(R) Macintosh and UNIX for Linux(R). On top of the operating system, specific applications are installed. General purpose operating systems allow a wide range of applications to be used. They do not necessarily allow the most efficient or fastest possible use of the hardware for the application.

Overlay: Keyed insertion of one image onto another.

PA: Crew members who are willing to do anything to gain experience. Most times the hardest workers on the set.

PAL: An acronym for phase alternating line. It is a composite color standard used in many parts of the world. The format consists of 625 scan lines of resolution at 25 fps (25 Hz). The phase alternation makes the signal less susceptible to distortion.

Pixel: The digital representation of the smallest area of a television capable of being delineated by the bit stream. The smaller and closer together the pixels the higher the picture resolution.

Plug-In: Additions to software that can be installed afterwards. Plug-ins provide special effects or features for respective software.

Post House: Abbreviation for post-production house. Mostly a company specialized in the business of cutting, color grading, finishing or conforming a clip, movie or film.

Post-Production: All production work performed after the raw video footage and audio elements have been captured. Editing, titles, special effects insertion image enhancement and audio mixing are done during post-production.

Prima Donna: Someone overly cocky yet clueless.

Primary Source Clip: A clip created from a source clip when the source clip is placed in the time line on the sequencer. It does not contain any digitized media. It only refers to the primary clip.

Production: Creation of recorded image information with associated audio elements to achieve the thematic and artistic content desired for distribution.

Production Sound: Audio recording during principle photography on-location.

Progressive Scanning: A display mode for electronic imaging in which all scanned lines are presented successively and each field has the same number of lines as a frame. It is also known as sequential scanning. It requires 2x the bandwidth of interlaced scanning.

Protocol: A set of syntax rules defining the exchange of data. Proxy: Material rendered in a lower quality, normally unsuitable for broadcast. Mainly used for preview or offline-editing purposes.

Pulldown: A technique that eliminates redundant frames when converting film material (24 fps) to NTSC (30 fps).

QuickTime: A QuickTime(R) file works as a multimedia container file. It contains one or more tracks, each of which stores a particular type of data, like video, audio, effects, or text (for subtitles, for example). Each track in turn contains track media. This might be either the digitally encoded media stream (using a specific codec, e.g. JPEG, MP3, DivX, or PNG or a data reference to the media stored in another file or elsewhere on a network. An edit list indicates what parts of the media to use.

RAID: RAID is an acronym for redundant array of independent disks. RAID is a method of enabling several physical hard disk drives to act as a single orchestrated storage device.

RAM: An acronym for random access memory. The chips in a computer that contain its working memory.

Raw Stock: Unexposed film or audiotape.

RCA Connector: A type of connector used on all VCRs and camcorders to carry standard composite video and audio signals. Also known as a phono connector.

Real Time: The idea or concept of a system that will react and respond as fast as things happen. A good example is to be seen within the games industry: moving the joystick and seeing the image on screen react simultaneously—the processes needed to achieve this effect are called real-time.

Record/Capture: Analog video (or audio) signals are converted into digital formats.

Reference Black Level: Refers to the horizontal timing discussion.

Reference Clip: A clip created from a source clip when the source clip is placed in the time line on the sequencer. Also known as a sub-clip and secondary clip.

Reference Genlock: Describes the process of signals being synchronized. When combining more than one signal, one specific reference signal will help to synchronize the different sources.

Release Print: Numerous duplicate prints of a subject made for general theatre release.

Remote Control: To control a system by remote. Most video systems can be controlled by remote, for example, via an RS-422 interface, a common control interface in the field of video equipment. With it you can, for instance, command a video system to start a play-out operation from another system, while recording the played out material at the same time with the foreign system. Tape machines such as VTRs can also be controlled that way, making simultaneous play-out and record operations between different systems an easy task. See also RS-422.

Rendering: The process by which video editing software and hardware convert raw video, effects, transitions, and filters into a new continuous video file. A non-real time drawing of a picture relying on computer processing speed for graphics and compositing.

Resolution: The sharpness or crispness of a picture. It can be measured numerically by establishing the number of scanning lines used to create each frame of video.

RF: An acronym for radio frequency. A term used to describe the radio signal band of the electromagnetic spectrum i.e. 3 MHz íŸí 300 GHz. RF connectors carry RF television signals.

RGB: The basic parallel component set (red; green; blue) in which a signal is used for each primary color. May also be referred to as GBR, the mechanical sequence of the connectors in the SMPTE interconnect standard.
ROM: An acronym for read only memory. Permanently programmed memory.

Rotation: An effect on a video system, which rotates and turns the images of a video clip at a freely definable angle. See also Effect.

Rough Cut: Assembly of edited shots before picture lock.

Routing: Describes the activity of a device within a computer network that will decide the destination of a data package. The router is connected to more than one network, is often included as part of a network switch.

RS-422: A medium range balanced serial data transmission standard. Full specification includes 9-way, D-type connectors. It is widely used for control links around production and post areas for a range of equipment.

Sampling: The process where analog signals are measured, often million of times per second in video, in order to convert analog signals to digital. The official sampling standard for television is ITU-R 601.

SAN: An acronym for storage area network.

SATA: An acronym for Serial ATA (advanced technology attachment). It is a further development of ATA also known as IDE. SATA is the successor of ATA, but it is a serial interface, resulting in easier cabling and fewer errors. The maximum data rate is 150 MB/sec. for SATA.

SATA-2: A newer version of SATA with a maximum data rate of 300 MB/sec.

Saturation: Term used to describe color brilliance or purity.

Scaling: Scaling generally indicates a change of the resolution of images, i.e. the images are made larger or smaller. Auto scaling is a setting of a video system that enables an automatic scaling and re-sizing of the original video material.

Scan Converter: An external device that converts a computer's VGA output to video so it can be displayed on a TV or VCR.

SCSI: An acronym for small computer system interface. It is a parallel interface that is used by computer systems to connect peripheral devices; a connection of up to 15 drives to one interface port.

SCSI Termination: A metal cap that plugs into any open SCSI port on a SCSI bus line. All SCSI ports need to be occupied by a cable or terminator to ensure proper function.

SD: An acronym for standard definition.

SDI: An acronym for serial digital interface. It is a standard based on 270 Mbps transfer rate. It is a 10-bit interface for both component and composite digital video with four (4) channels of embedded digital audio. It uses 75-Ohm BNC connectors and coax cable and can transmit signal over 600 feet.

Serial Port: A computer input/output (I/O) port through which the computer communicates with the external environment. The standard serial port uses RS-232 and RS-422 protocols.

Server: When a computer provides services to other computing systems (clients) over a network, it is defined as a server. Most complex computer systems today require a server, but the term can also refer to the software or hardware elements of such a system.

Shortcut: Two types of shortcuts: 1. Computer shortcuts are small files containing the location of other files. Computer shortcuts are usually located on the desktop to start programs without using a command line. 2. Keyboard shortcut describes a key or set of keys to perform a predefined function. Sequences such as using a menu or typing commands can be reduced to a few keystrokes.

Shuttle: Functionality: 1.Viewing footage at speeds greater than real time. 2. A removable drive unit for easy transport of data and media files from one system to another without connecting and disconnecting cables.

Signal to Noise Ratio (S/N): The ratio between the strength of an electronic signal and the amount of electronic background noise. S/N is measured in decibels (dB). Video specifications include three (3) figures: Video (luminance); Color (chrominance); Audio (sound). The larger the ratio the better the signal.

SMART: SMART is an acronym for self-monitoring analysis and reporting technology. It allows disk drives to perform sophisticated self-diagnosis and auto-correction when possible and reports faults to the computer's operating system (OS) when necessary.

SMTP: An acronym for simple mail transfer protocol which is a TCP/IP protocol. In sending and receiving email it is usually used with POP3 or IMAP protocols to generate a user-friendly emailing process. SMTP is typically used by programs for sending email while either POP3 or IMAP support programs for receiving email.

SMPTE: SMPTE is an acronym for Society of Motion Picture & Television Engineers. This group establishes and enforces industry technical standards.

Source Clip: Refers directly to physical media.

Source Timecode: Timecode information stored directly in the video clip or the individual frames of an image sequence (stored in the file headers). See also Timecode.

Split Edit: A type of edit transition where either the video or the audio is delayed from being recorded for a given time.

Split-Screen: An effect that displays two images separated by a horizontal or vertical wipe line.

Squeeze: A change in the aspect ratio. Anamorphic lenses sometimes squeeze a widescreen scene by a factor of 2 horizontally so it will fit on a 1.33:1 aspect ratio frame.

Stand-Alone: Stand-alone describes programs which run without the services of other programs (except maybe firmware).

Standard Definition Image: 720 x 470

Stereo: Stereophonic sound. Two independent audio channels are used to create a spatial sound effect.

S-Video: An abbreviation for separated video. The standard for the way a signal is carried on the cable itself. S-Video is a hardware standard that defines the physical cable jacks. The industry has settled on a 4-pin mini-plug connector. S-Video has no relationship to the resolution or refresh-rate of the signal.

Sweetening: The final combining and enhancing of a video program's audio tracks.

Sync Sound: Sound recorded with the intention of being married to a picture at an exact point.

Synchronization: Also referred to as sync. It is a transmission procedure by which the bit and character streams are controlled by accurately synchronized clocks, both at the receiving and sending end.

TBC: Time base corrector. A device used to correct for time base errors and stabilize the timing of the video output from a tape machine. It corrects problems in a video signals sync-pulse by generating a new, clean time-base and synchronizes any other incoming video to this reference.

TCP: An acronym for transport control protocol. It is the major transport protocol in the Internet suite of protocols providing reliable, connection-oriented, full-duplex streams. It uses IP for delivery.

Telecine: The process of transferring film data to videotape.

Terabyte: Equivalent to 1 trillion bytes or 1 thousand gigabytes.

Third-Party: Software or hardware developed by other manufacturers.

Thumbnail: A down-converted image to provide a preview of its original material. Thumbnails are used to show the contents of video clips in still images. Thus, a complete loading and play-out of the clip only to take a look at its contents is not necessary.

TIFF: An acronym for tag image file format. It is the standard file format for high-resolution bit-mapped graphics. TIFF files may be compressed or uncompressed.

Timecode: A system for numbering video frames where a code denoting hours/minutes/seconds/frames is assigned to each frame. In North America, the timecode standard is SMPTE.

Timecode Generator: A signal generator designed to generate and transmit SMPTE timecode.

Timeline: The graphic representation of a program displayed in the sequencer window.

Tracking: The angle and speed at which the tape passes the video heads.

Transcoder: A device that converts one component format to another, e.g. to convert Y, R-Y, B-Y signals to RGB signals.

Transition: A change from one clip to the next. A popular example is a cut, when the first frame of the starting video segment directly follows the last frame of the segment that is ending. Other transitions are dissolves, wipes, fades, or DVEs.

Trim: The adjusting of transitions in a sequence.

Trim Handles: The frames before or after the in and out points for a source clip allowing for trimming and transitions.

Uncompressed: Uncompressing (or decompressing) is the act of expanding a compression file back into its original form. Software often comes in a compressed package, e.g. as Internet download. It often decompresses itself when you click on it. Files can be uncompressed using popular tools such as PKZIP in the DOS operating system, WinZip in Windows, and Mac Zip in Macintosh.

Up-Conversion: The process of converting low-resolution video to higher resolution video.

USB: An acronym for universal serial bus.

Vectorscope: A specialized oscilloscope, which demodulates the video signal and presents a display of R-Y versus B-Y. It allows for the accurate evaluation of the chrominance portion of a signal.

Vertical Interval: The vertical interval signals the picture monitor to go back to the top of the screen to begin another vertical scan. It is the portion of the video signal that occurs between the end of one field and the beginning of the next.

Video Clip: In a non-linear editing environment, a clip indicates data of either video or audio that has been clipped out (copied) from a larger environment such as a reel or videotape. In essence, a video clip is a snippet of video. Video clips usually are folders/directories that contain a great number of individual image files (the frames), which combined form the video sequence. The image files can be stored in a wide variety of picture file formats (e.g. BMP or TIFF). However, video clips can also be stored in a single file in a container file format such as QuickTime or Windows Media.

Video Format: Determines the way video is transmitted or received. For example, for a record it determines how to receive a video signal at the inputs. Most notably the setting of a video format must detail the video raster (resolution, e.g. 1920)

Video Switcher: A device that allows transmissions between different video pictures. May contain special effects generators.

Volume: An identifiable unit of data storage in computers or storage systems. It might be physically removable. In tape storage systems, a volume may be a tape cartridge (or in older systems, a tape reel). In mainframe storage systems, a volume may be a removable hard disk. Each volume can be specified by the user via its system-unique name or number. In some systems, the physical unit may be divided into several separately identifiable volumes.

VTR: An acronym for video tape recorder.

VU: An abbreviation for volume units. A unit of measure for complex audio signals, usually in decibels (dB). The reference level of -20 dB is 0 VU.

WAV: An abbreviation for wave, i.e. the wave file format. File format for digital audio (waveform) data under Windows that can be used for audio clips. It is capable of storing multiple mono or stereo channels.

Waveform Monitor: A specialized oscilloscope that displays analog video signals at a horizontal and/or vertical rate. It is used for evaluating television signals.

Window Dub: Copies of videotape with burnt-in timecode display. Hours, minutes, seconds, and frames appear on the recorded image.

Windows: Operating system for IBM compatible PCs developed by the company Microsoft®.

Wipe: A shaped transition between video sources. A margin or border moves across the screen, wiping out the image of one scene and replacing it with an image of the next scene.

WMV: Microsoft developed a set of video codec technologies called Windows Media Video. WMV is part of the Windows® Media framework.

Work Print: Any picture or sound track print, usually positive, intended for use in the editing process to establish the finished version of a film.

Workflow: Workflow is the operational aspect of a work procedure. It describes how tasks are structured, who performs them, what their relative order is, how they are synchronized, how information flows to support the tasks, and how tasks are being tracked. As dimension of time, workflow considers throughput as a distinct measure.

Workstation: A high-end, specialized computer system intended for use by engineers or imaging professionals.

XFR: A slang expression for transfer.

XLR: A secure three (3) pronged audio-connector covered by a metal sheath often found on high quality audio/video equipment; a type of audio connector featuring three leads: two for the signal and one for overall system grounding. XLR is often used for microphones.

Y, U, V: Luminance and color difference components for the PAL system. Y, U, and V are simply new names for Y, R-Y, and B-Y. The derivation from RGB is identical.

YUV: YUV is the abbreviation for the differential brightness and color signals. It is the color space used by NTSC and PAL video systems. While the Y is the luma component, the U and V are the color difference components. Some may mistake the Y'U'V notation for Y'CbCr data. Most use the YUV notation rather than Y'UV or Y'U'V'. Technically correct is Y'U'V' since all three components are derived from RGB. YUV is also the name for some component analog interfaces of consumer equipment.

Zero Timing Point: The point at which all video signals must be in synchronization, typically the switcher input.

Zipper Head: A person who has no common sense or logic.

Zoom and Pan: Zoom increases the length of the camera lens, magnifying an aspect of a scene. The results of a zoom and a dolly are different. A dolly physically moves the camera closer to the point of interest without changing the length of the lens. Zoom increases the size of the point of interest by increasing the lens length.

About the Author

Kevin DiBacco has more than thirty years' experience as a music video, documentary film and feature film director. Kevin has four motion pictures in various phases of worldwide distribution. Currently, he is consulting on the feature film, "One," starring Lance Henriksen. Kevin is also is the author of *The Real World Guide to Digital Filmmaking*, published by Keith Publications (2017), *The Artist Toolkit,* and the recently completed manuscript, *Gabardine Gang.* Kevin also consults on motion picture production and distribution for other producers and filmmakers in the business. Not only does Kevin know film and video production he has developed an inside understanding about the film business, which most filmmakers do not have. To date, Kevin has secured distribution deals for more than ten different feature films for filmmakers around the country.

For more information,
www.kevindibacco.com
www.themadmoviemaker.com
www.dibaccofilms.com
kdibacco@me.com
dibaccofilms@me.com

www.keithpublications.com

CPSIA information can be obtained
at www.ICGtesting.com
Printed in the USA
BVOW09s1930141117
500153BV00008B/147/P